*Sports Fundamentals Series*

# SOFTBALL
*Fundamentals*

*Rick Noren*
Pacific Lutheran University

**Human Kinetics**

Library of Congress Cataloging-in-Publication Data

Noren, Rick.
    Softball fundamentals / Rick Noren.
      p. cm. -- (Sports fundamentals series)
    ISBN 0-7360-5584-3
    1. Softball. I. Human Kinetics (Organization) II. Title. III. Series.
    GV881.N62 2005
    796.357'8--dc22                          2004026208

ISBN: 0-7360-5584-3

**Acquisitions Editor:** Jana Hunter; **Developmental Editors:** Susanna Blalock, Cynthia McEntire; **Assistant Editors:** Cory Weber, Kim Thoren; **Copyeditor:** Patricia MacDonald; **Proofreader:** Kathy Bennett; **Graphic Designer:** Robert Reuther; **Graphic Artist:** Kim McFarland; **Photo Manager:** Dan Wendt; **Cover Designer:** Keith Blomberg; **Photographer (interior):** Kelly Huff; **Art Manager:** Kareema McLendon; **Illustrator:** Argosy; **Printer:** United Graphics

We thank Pacific Lutheran University in Tacoma, Washington, for assistance in providing the location for the photo shoot for this book.

Human Kinetics books are available at special discounts for bulk purchase. Special editions or book excerpts can also be created to specification. For details, contact the Special Sales Manager at Human Kinetics.

Printed in the United States of America     10   9   8   7   6   5   4   3   2   1

**Human Kinetics**
Web site: www.HumanKinetics.com

*United States:* Human Kinetics
P.O. Box 5076
Champaign, IL 61825-5076
800-747-4457
e-mail: humank@hkusa.com

*Canada:* Human Kinetics
475 Devonshire Road Unit 100
Windsor, ON N8Y 2L5
800-465-7301 (in Canada only)
e-mail: orders@hkcanada.com

*Europe:* Human Kinetics
107 Bradford Road
Stanningley
Leeds LS28 6AT, United Kingdom
+44 (0) 113 255 5665
e-mail: hk@hkeurope.com

*Australia:* Human Kinetics
57A Price Avenue
Lower Mitcham, South Australia 5062
08 8277 1555
e-mail: liaw@hkaustralia.com

*New Zealand:* Human Kinetics
Division of Sports Distributors NZ Ltd.
P.O. Box 300 226 Albany
North Shore City
Auckland
0064 9 448 1207
e-mail: blairc@hknewz.com

# Welcome to Sports Fundamentals

The Sports Fundamentals Series uses a learn-by-doing approach to teach those who want to play, not just read. Clear, concise instructions and illustrations make it easy to become more proficient in the game or activity, allowing readers to participate quickly and have more fun.

Between the covers, this book contains rock-solid information, precise instructions, and clear photos and illustrations that immerse readers in the sport. Each fundamental chapter is divided into four major sections:

- You Can Do It!: Jump right into the game or activity with a clear explanation of how to perform an essential skill or tactic.
- More to Choose and Use: Find out more about the skill, or learn exciting alternatives.
- Take It to the Field: Apply the new skill in a game situation.
- Give It a Go: Use drills and gamelike activities to develop skills by doing; gauge learning and performance with self-tests.

No more sitting on the sidelines! The Sports Fundamentals Series gets you right into the game. Apply the techniques and tactics as they are learned, and have fun—win or lose!

# Contents

# Introduction

Developing the fundamentals of fastpitch softball can lay the groundwork for a lifetime of involvement. By mastering the fundamental skills, you can play the game just for fun or possibly compete at an elite level.

Fastpitch softball requires individual skills within the framework of a team. One of the sport's greatest attributes is that teammates must work together to be successful. To play the game, athletes don't need to be tall, as in basketball or volleyball, or as fit as a cross country runner. Each position requires different abilities, and players of all shapes and sizes can find a place on the field to play.

Although very similar to the game of baseball, fastpitch softball enjoys some dramatic differences. Games are usually played at a much quicker pace than baseball, and although men do play fastpitch, it is played predominantly by female athletes. Let's develop an understanding of the basic rules of the game before getting started with the fundamental skills.

## Field and Equipment

Although it looks very similar to a baseball field, the fastpitch softball field is significantly smaller. Usually the outfield fences range from 190 feet (57.9 meters) to 220 feet (67.1 meters) away from home plate. The bases are 60 feet (18.3 meters) apart, rather than 90 feet (27.4 meters) as on a baseball diamond. In high school competition and most junior leagues, the pitcher throws from a distance of 40 feet (12.2 meters) away from home plate (figure 1). In college competition, the distance is moved back another three feet, to 43 feet (13.1 meters) from the pitcher to home plate.

The type and style of uniform vary depending on the age group and the type of team. For junior programs, especially those that operate during the warm summer months, shorts and a T-shirt are common. Collegiate teams may wear shorts, but because of the weather many wear pants, long undershirts, and heavier tops. Team members should wear matching uniforms as well as visors or hats, if desired. Sliding shorts, a tight-fitting garment worn under the uniform, and

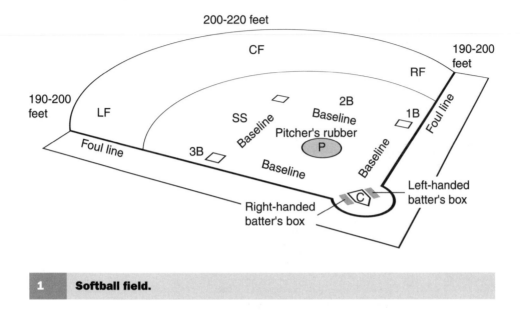

200-220 feet

CF

190-200 feet

RF

190-200 feet

LF

SS

Baseline

2B

Baseline

1B

Foul line

Baseline

Pitcher's rubber

3B

P

Baseline

Baseline

Foul line

Baseline

Left-handed batter's box

Right-handed batter's box

C

**1**    **Softball field.**

kneepads can reduce injuries on the field (e.g., sliding shorts can prevent skin abrasions during sliding).

Young players wear rubber cleats to help them dig into the dirt and grass for improved traction. Older players wear metal cleats, which provide a little more traction but increase the likelihood of injury when sliding into another player.

Some players wear batting gloves to get a better grip on the bat. A batting helmet should be worn from the time the batter enters the playing field until the batter returns to the bench area. Many players also wear face masks to prevent facial injuries from the ball.

Virtually all players use a bat made of an aluminum alloy, and bats are tested regularly for safety. The ball is 12 inches (30 centimeters) in diameter. Different manufacturers create balls that have a different feel—players can use the type of ball they prefer. In the past several years, the ball has changed color, going from white to an optic yellow with red seams. The new color helps batters see the ball better and results in a greater offensive game.

Another necessary piece of equipment is the glove. For most players, a five-fingered fielder's glove, ranging in size from 11 to 13 inches (28 to 33 centimeters), is customary (figure 2). An infielder typically uses a smaller glove so she can get the ball out of the glove more quickly to make a quick throw. A first baseman can use a mitt that has the fingers stitched together and a larger pocket for receiving throws at first base. The catcher also might wear a different mitt with extra padding to protect the hand from the impact of the pitch.

2 **A fielder's mitt, a catcher's mitt, and a first baseman's mitt.**

# Rules

One of the advantages of playing fastpitch softball is that the number of players involved in a game can be flexible. Typically 10 players make up a team, including 3 outfielders, 4 infielders, a pitcher, a catcher, and a designated, or extra, player. The designated player is allowed to bat for one of the defensive players, but she can go into the game and play defensively for another player as well.

A player who starts the game and is substituted for can reenter the game one time. The substitute player is out of the game once she is removed from the lineup.

Players must always bat in the order turned in to the umpire at the beginning of the game. If an offensive team bats out of order, the defensive team can take the result of the play or choose to have an out recorded.

In each inning, the offensive team tries to score as many runs as possible before three outs are recorded. To keep the game enjoyable for both teams, some junior leagues put a restriction on the number of runs per inning a team can score. For leagues playing under this rule, the inning is over when the defensive team records three outs or the offensive team reaches its run allotment.

While making contact with the ball, the batter must stay inside the batter's box. However, the batter can be in motion while making contact, as long as she is within the batter's box. (The left-handed slap hit, page 86, is one such play.) Once the batter puts the ball in play, she tries to reach first base before the defensive player covering first receives the ball from the defense and touches the base. The batter is free to try to reach additional bases but is at risk of being thrown out by the defense.

When the batter puts the ball in play, the defensive team tries to field the hit and get the ball to first base. If the ball reaches first base and the covering player touches the base before the batter reaches it, the batter is out. This is an example of a force play. In a force play, the runner is forced to a certain base. All the defensive team needs to do is get the ball to the player covering the base, who then touches the bag. When a play is not a force play, the defensive player with the ball must tag the runner, not just touch the base. A steal is an example of a non-force play.

The defensive team in the field can get an out by catching a hit ball before it hits the ground, catching a foul ball before it hits the ground, forcing a batter out at a base, or tagging a runner who is off a base. The pitcher can get an out by striking out the batter.

An umpire stands behind the catcher and calls each pitch that isn't hit either a ball or a strike. A strike is called if the ball passes over home plate between the batter's knees and her chest (figure 3), if the batter fouls off the pitch, or if the batter swings at the pitch and misses. Any pitch that doesn't fall within the strike zone is called a ball, unless the batter swings at the pitch. If the batter gets four balls, she goes to first base; any runners already on base advance to the next base. If the batter gets three strikes, she is out. If the batter fouls the pitch on what would have been strike three, she gets to continue the at-bat.

3　Strike zone.

The pitcher takes position on the pitcher's plate before beginning the motion. In high school and junior leagues, only one foot must be in contact with the plate (figure 4a). In college and Olympic play, both feet must be in contact with the plate (figure 4b). The catcher sets up behind home plate to receive the pitch. The catcher must remain within the confines of the catcher's box during the pitch. All other defensive players can position themselves anywhere on the field as long as they are within the foul lines.

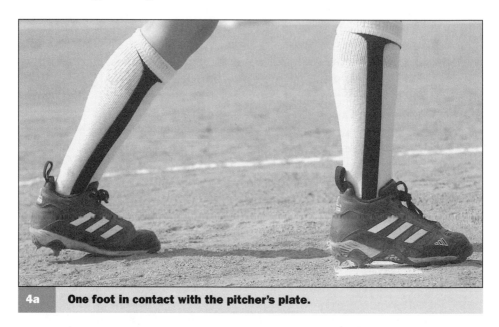

**4a**    **One foot in contact with the pitcher's plate.**

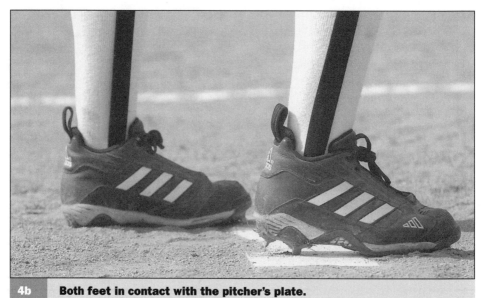

**4b**    **Both feet in contact with the pitcher's plate.**

Now that you know the basic idea of the game, it's time to learn the fundamental skills and get started on the path of becoming a better fastpitch player.

# Warm-Up

As with any sport, for softball it is important to prepare your body by warming up. Walk or jog slowly for a few minutes to increase your heart rate and warm your muscles.

After moving continuously for a few minutes, your muscles should be ready to stretch. For most athletes, a simple static stretching program is a great way to prepare for activity. For a static stretch, hold the stretch for about 30 seconds per exercise. Remember to stretch muscles only until they feel tight. Otherwise you could injure yourself. Breathe comfortably, and try to relax while stretching. Allow the muscles to elongate in preparation for the activity. Slowly stretch the targeted muscle, and don't bounce or jerk during the stretch—forcing the muscle to do too much can cause injury.

Stretch the large muscle groups of the legs, back, hips, and shoulders thoroughly before beginning activity. Sit on the ground with your legs together and straight. Reach toward your toes until you feel a stretch in the back of your legs, your back, and your shoulders (figure 5).

**5**     **Straight-leg stretch.**

While still seated on the ground, bend one knee and put that leg over the other. Rest your foot on the ground. Place the opposite elbow on the bent knee, and turn your body so you are looking behind you. You should feel a tightness in your back and shoulders (figure 6).

**8**    Torso stretch.

Next get into a kneeling position on both knees. Slowly lean back, catching yourself with your hands. Push your hips forward until you feel a tightness in the front of your legs (figure 7).

**7**    **Quad stretch.**

A good shoulder and arm warm-up is arm circles. Stand and extend your arms out to your sides, palms up. Move your arms in small circles (figure 8). Keep the arms straight by locking your elbows. Gradually increase the size of the circles until your shoulders begin to tire. Rest for a few seconds, then do arm circles in the other direction by making circles that go backward.

8    **Arm circles.**

# Key to Diagrams

| | |
|---|---|
| Left fielder | LF |
| Right fielder | RF |
| Centerfielder | CF |
| Shortstop | SS |
| First baseman | 1B |
| Second baseman | 2B |
| Third baseman | 3B |
| Pitcher | P |
| Catcher | C |
| Throw/hit (ball flight) | - - - - ▸ |
| Running path | ⟶ |
| Player 1, player 2, etc. | $X_1$, $X_2$ |
| Player with the ball | ⓧ |
| Batter | B |
| Runner | R |
| Target 1, target 2, etc. | $T_1$, $T_2$ |

# Throwing

One of the body's earliest and most natural movements is the act of throwing, as evidenced when an infant grabs a block and tosses it across the room for the first time. However the development of speed and accuracy in a throw takes years of practice and proper instruction.

Making a perfect throw late in a pressure-packed game can be a tremendous mental as well as physical challenge. The confidence necessary to perform in these situations comes from both developing the proper throwing mechanics and endless hours of practice. Whether participating in a recreational or competitive setting, perfecting the correct fundamentals can also be critical for preventing shoulder and arm injuries. By developing sound techniques early in the learning process, and by implementing a well-designed warm-up program, the risk of injury from the repetitive motion can be reduced and the potential for improvement greatly increased.

# Throw It!

Throwing accuracy begins with the grip. Start by holding the ball with your middle finger on the threads and your thumb on the opposite side of the ball. Then lay each of your other fingers comfortably on the seams, with your pinkie finger resting on the outside (figure 1.1). This grip will enable you to apply proper rotation and added velocity to the ball, as well as keep it balanced and stable during the throw. A ball that has perfect backspin will travel straight and cut through the air more easily. Watch the ball to see how it spins; if your middle finger is the last point of contact, the ball should spin nice and straight. If you have difficulty seeing the ball spin, put a piece of black tape around the ball. Keep a relaxed grip on the ball, as if holding an egg you don't want to drop or break. This will give you maximum wrist flexibility at release.

To develop throwing velocity, take a small step to gain balance, and align your shoulders and hips to the target by pivoting on that foot. Next bring the ball and glove hand up above the shoulders into a position similar to a conductor leading an orchestra (figure 1.2a). Transfer your weight by taking a step toward the target, and bring the ball forward, releasing it by snapping the wrist (figure 1.2b). The

**1.1**   **Grip the ball.**

wrist snap allows you to throw the ball with greater velocity. It will look similar to a windshield wiper on a car. The ball begins in a cocked position, and as your wrist snaps forward the ball is released.

To prevent injury, follow through with your arm and leg after you release the ball. The most common injuries are pulled muscles and sore elbows; however, greater damage that may require surgery may occur if improper technique is used.

Watch the flight of the ball. See how it spins on the way to the target. If it tends to spin sideways and travel away from the intended target, adjust your release so that the ball leaves the middle finger last, thereby creating proper backspin.

As you become more proficient with the proper throwing mechanics, the movements should become quicker and more fluid. Eventually the pause in the conductor position will no longer be required. Instead it will be replaced with a continuous motion of the hands working together. In addition, using the large muscles of the torso and legs will improve the velocity of the throw as well as reduce injuries to the shoulder and arm.

**1.2a**    **Raise ball and glove to above shoulders.**    **1.2b**    **Transfer your weight.**

During game situations, an alternative throwing motion may be necessary depending on the circumstance. Distance to the target, the need for a quicker release, or the necessity of throwing on the run are a few examples. This section explores several of these options. As with any skill, it is important to practice each option before using it in a game situation.

**Dart Throw**    The dart throw is a simple, quick throw that is useful for short distances. Once again, the grip is important and should be the same as for the standard throw. Hold the ball high near the ear; the ball should be clearly visible to the recipient in anticipation of a quick throw (figure 1.3a). Because the distance of this throw is typically short, accuracy rather than velocity is critical. A quick forward movement of the forearm, followed by the snapping of the wrist at release, propels the ball toward the target (figure 1.3b). Very little movement or weight transfer is necessary for this type of throw.

## Dart Throw

| 1.3a | Hold ball up near the ear. | 1.3b | Snap the wrist at release. |

**Sidearm Release**  Another throwing variation is the sidearm release. The sidearm can be used for short, quick throws. Typically a sidearm throw is used at second base to begin a double play or when attempting to throw out a quick runner. As with the dart throw, the velocity for the sidearm release comes from the arm movement and wrist snap. Lightly grasp the ball with the fingers and draw it back behind your hip (figure 1.4a). Keep the elbow close to the body, and propel the ball toward the target with a whipping action of the forearm and wrist (figure 1.4b). After releasing the ball, follow through with the arm across the body in order to decelerate the arm.

**Sidearm Release**

| 1.4a | **Bring ball back behind hip.** | 1.4b | **Whip forearm and wrist to propel ball.** |

## Throwing on the Run

Occasionally it will be necessary to make a throw while on the run (e.g., when fielding a bunted ball and throwing across the diamond). As you secure the ball in your throwing hand, take a step with the foot on the same side as the throwing hand (figure 1.5a). Use a short arm motion to deliver the ball to the target (figure 1.5b). Without a stationary foundation to generate power on the throw, you need to generate a quick release (figure 1.5c). Although throwing on the run generally involves only a short throw, accuracy is difficult. Becoming proficient at this throw requires a great deal of practice.

### Throwing on the Run

**1.5a** Step with foot on throwing-hand side.

**1.5c** Quick release.

**1.5b** Short arm motion.

**Underhand Toss**   For very short throws that require a quick release, the underhand toss may be the best choice. While similar to
the other throwing variations, the underhand toss typically uses a
straight-arm delivery. Usually you pick up the ball with the throwing
hand, and in the same motion, bring it back a short distance behind
the hip (figure 1.6a). Keep the arm straight as it moves forward in
a pendulum motion toward the target. Release the ball by snapping
the wrist, allowing the ball to roll off the pads of the fingers (figure
1.6b). For this throw, however, the palm of the hand will be turned
up during the follow-through.

**Underhand Toss**

| 1.6a | Bring ball behind hip with throwing hand. | 1.6b | Snap the wrist at release. |

# Choosing Throws

The game of softball requires a variety of skills. Because the game is played from all parts of the field and situations constantly change, throwing a ball accurately is a requisite skill for any player. When you consider the variety of situations that arise in a game, you can understand how developing an accurate throw to use in each specific case is difficult. After becoming proficient with the standard throwing motion, be sure to practice the numerous variations for your position.

Outfielders will use the standard throw (see figure 1.2, page 3) the vast majority of the time. Some situations, however, require the outfielder to charge the ball and quickly release it on the run.

Players in infield positions must master a variety of throws. Long throws are typically not necessary because of the infielders' proximity to the bases. An infielder relies on a quick release to cover the short distance the ball needs to travel. A first baseman may use an underhand throw to toss a fielded ground ball to the player covering first base. A shortstop or second baseman may use a sidearm throw to quickly release the ball at the beginning of a double play. A third baseman might use either of these throwing variations, depending on the situation. He might use an underhand toss if a batter bunts the ball and a runner is heading toward home or when the shortstop is covering third base. If the shortstop is going to make a play at first base after fielding a bunt, she may need to throw on the run. Infielders use the dart throw primarily during rundowns because this throw allows them to release the ball quickly, but the receiving player can easily see the ball coming.

Practice all these throwing variations to ensure success in a game. It is difficult to anticipate when a certain throw will be required, but with experience and practice, you can learn when and how to perform the necessary throws.

Developing an accurate throw can be a lengthy and time-consuming process. By breaking the motion into segments and practicing these smaller pieces, the overall skill can be learned more quickly. Progressing through these drills on a daily basis builds a solid foundation for throwing accurately and quickly. These drills also serve as an important warm-up for throwing during a game.

## BALL SPIN DRILL

Learning to throw a ball with proper spin is critical for an accurate throw. Wrap tape around the ball through the center so that it bisects the horseshoe-shaped seams. Grip the ball so that the pad of your middle finger rests on the line at the seam and your thumb rests on the line opposite the middle finger. Place the pads of the index and ring fingers on the seams, and place the pinkie along the outside of the ball to help stabilize it.

Lie on your back and hold your elbow in the air, keeping it in line with your shoulder (figure 1.7a). Bring the ball toward your ear. Throw the ball by first unlocking your elbow and then your wrist. The ball should spin backward off your middle finger as you release it, similar to shooting a basketball (figure 1.7b). If the ball is spinning correctly, the taped line will spin straight. Initially toss the ball only a couple of feet in the air. Gradually toss the ball higher as you become more proficient.

For a two-player variation of this drill, stand facing a partner. Toss the ball back and forth, keeping your elbow still at shoulder height, supporting the throwing arm with the opposite hand. Once again, the goal is to spin the ball so that the taped line stays straight.

**1.7** **Ball spin drill.**

## ONE-KNEE DRILL

Wrap tape around the ball through the center so that it bisects the horseshoe-shaped seams. Stand approximately 15 feet (4.6 meters) away from your partner, and kneel on your throwing-side knee. (Your partner should kneel as well.) Your other knee should point toward your partner. This position allows you to isolate upper body motion during the throw. Using the proper grip, prepare to release the ball by holding it in the conductor position (see figure 1.2a, page 3). Use the basic throwing motion to send the ball to your partner (figure 1.8). Watch for the taped line to spin straight as the ball goes to your partner. Emphasize the rotation of the shoulders, and follow through across the body on the throw.

**1.8** **One-knee drill.**

## FOUR-CORNER DRILL

The four-corner drill requires at least four players and a regulation softball field with bases. A player stands in front of each base. The player at home plate starts the drill by throwing the ball to the player at third base. The player at third base then throws the ball to the player at second base. The player at second base throws the ball to the player at first base, who throws it to the player at home plate. Continue this ball rotation around the infield for a specific period of time and then reverse the rotation, throwing the ball in the other direction around the infield.

## STAR DRILL

The star drill requires at least 10 players divided into five groups. Each group represents the point of an imaginary star (figure 1.9). One group has a ball. The first player in this group throws the ball to the first player in the line two groups to the left, then runs to the end of the line she threw to. The receiver then throws the ball to the first player in the line two groups to the left, then runs to the end of this line, and so on around the star. Continue the motion until someone drops the ball.

The star drill is repeated in the next chapter, but here the focus is on throwing the ball with accuracy, and in the next chapter the focus is on catching the ball.

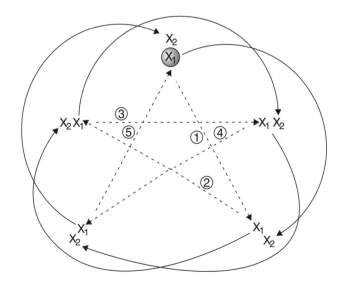

**1.9** **Star drill.**

# Catching

**D**uring the early years of baseball and softball, players didn't use a glove to field the ball, so it was vital that they learned to catch the ball properly. They needed to use both their hands and "give" with the ball as they caught it to cushion the blow.

Today players use a leather glove to catch with, and some gloves are almost two feet (.6 meters) long. Because of this change, most players now use only one hand to catch the ball, increasing the likelihood of dropping the ball at a crucial time during a game.

Have you ever heard someone say, "She tried to throw it before she caught it"? Well there isn't going to be a throw unless you catch the ball in the first place. Many players take the art of catching a ball for granted, but if you've ever made the mistake of dropping the ball during a game, you know that feeling of embarrassment will last for quite a while. Although errors will always be part of the game, with practice and careful study of the information in this chapter, you will be able to improve your catching ability.

# Catch It!

It would be great if every throw that came your way was straight and ended up about chest high. All you would have to do is put your glove up and the ball would land right in the pocket. Unfortunately it seldom works that way. To be good at catching the ball, you must learn to be ready for anything.

Although the glove is vital when catching the ball, it is just as important to learn proper footwork. Catching the ball begins with seeing the ball, then reacting to its location by moving your feet.

Stand in a good athletic position, ready to move in any direction. A good athletic position (figure 2.1a) begins with your feet slightly wider than your shoulders, knees slightly bent, weight on the balls of your feet. Bend slightly at the waist so that your shoulders are directly above your knees. This position will enable you to react quickly in any direction.

Even if you know the tendencies of the player about to throw you the ball, be sure to watch the thrower carefully as she releases it. Watch the release and spin of the ball so you can react more quickly if the throw is off target. Move your feet quickly toward where you think the ball is going to end up (figure 2.1b). As you run, stay on the balls of your feet and take short, choppy steps. Keep your knees bent so you can bend down or jump up as needed.

**2.1a** Begin in athletic position.

**2.1b** Move feet quickly to get in position.

Once you are in position, extend your glove arm toward the on-coming ball until your arm is nearly straight (figure 2.1c). At this point, watch the ball intently so that your eye–hand coordination takes over and you can move the glove to the ball.

Just as the ball enters the glove, smoothly give with the force of the ball by bending your elbow (figure 2.1d). Called having "soft hands," this will stop the ball more gently, giving you a better chance of keeping it in the glove. If you keep your arm straight and stiff, the ball will collide with the glove like something hitting a brick wall. As you squeeze the leather glove around the ball, bring your throwing hand to the glove and cover the ball to make sure it doesn't pop out. This not only helps avoid some of those costly errors but also puts you in position to quickly grab the ball for the next throw.

Ideally, make the catch just in front of your throwing-hand shoulder. This allows for an easy transition to the throwing position. It is also helpful to move your feet into the throwing position as you catch the ball, but remember the most important thing is to catch the ball first. You can't throw it until you catch it.

**2.1c** Extend glove arm toward ball.

**2.1d** Bend elbow while catching ball in glove.

Because fielding gloves rather than bare hands are used to catch the ball, there are some dos and don'ts for positioning the glove, depending on where the ball goes. Although these skills are primarily used by infielders, it is important that every player be able to react to a throw that is a little off target.

**Above the Waist**   Since the target for the incoming throw is the shoulder, most of the time you will catch the ball above the waist. When catching the ball above the waist, be sure to remain in athletic position, and position the glove with the fingers pointing up (figure 2.2). Having the glove pocket open will make it easier for you to adjust to the ball in different locations above the waist. This glove position also makes it easier to move your feet into throwing position as you catch the ball.

**2.2**   **Fingers point up when catching above the waist.**

**Below the Waist**   Reacting to a throw that is below your waist begins by lowering your center of gravity while staying in athletic position. As the ball approaches and you realize it is going to be low, bend your knees. Maintain your balance with a wide stance. Watch the ball into your glove. Place your hands out in front of your body, and turn your glove so that the fingers point down (figure 2.3). As the ball enters the glove, give with your elbow and cover up the ball with your throwing hand. Keep your knees bent and stay low until the ball is secure. If you stand up too early and take your eyes off the ball, you are more likely to drop it. Catching the ball below the waist is not difficult, although it will take more time to get back into throwing position. It is important not to rush; rushing could result in an error.

**2.3**   **Fingers point down when catching below the waist.**

**Over the Head** When reacting to a high throw, point the fingers of the glove up. You may need to stretch out your arm or even jump off the ground for a very high throw. When catching a throw above your head, use only the glove hand. You can reach higher if you stretch out only your glove arm. Jump to try to reach a throw that appears to be sailing over your head. Start in a good athletic position, which will help you jump by providing more balance and a powerful push-off. As you jump into the air, raise your arms and concentrate on watching the ball into the glove (figure 2.4). After making the catch, cover the ball with your throwing hand to keep it secure. Your primary goal with a very high throw is just to catch and secure the ball. It will take more time to get into throwing position, but you have a chance as long as you make the catch.

**2.4** **Over the head.**

# Catching Tactics

"Defense wins championships" is a common proverb in sports. This couldn't be more true than in the game of softball. Although pitching is certainly the dominating factor for successful teams, not far behind is the ability to play error-free defense.

In its simplest form, good defense comes down to a team being able to play catch. It is rare for a player to miss a perfectly thrown ball, but it is a different story when throws are slightly off target. Since outfielders typically don't cover a base, it would be unusual for an outfielder to catch a throw during a game. However every infield position, including the pitcher and catcher, must be able to handle difficult throws.

The position that most often has to deal with poor throws is first base. Because a high percentage of outs occurs at first, the first baseman must be able to reach both low throws in the dirt and high throws over the head. Having a tall first baseman can be a defensive advantage, allowing a little more room for error on high throws. The first baseman also must be tough minded to handle low throws that bounce in the dirt. A first baseman is expected to not only catch every poorly thrown ball but also do it with one foot in contact with the base.

Other infield positions also require the ability to make difficult catches, but not as frequently. More commonly, other infielders must catch a ball while on the run and either touch a base or tag the runner. The shortstop and second baseman must cover a great deal more space, so timing the arrival at the base and the catch of the oncoming ball can be a difficult task. While making a catch on the run, it is important to concentrate on the ball first and then worry about the next aspect of the play. Whether you simply need to touch the base and get out of the runner's way or stop and make a tag as the runner slides, you still need to catch the ball first. Too often a player loses sight of the ball for a split second and then misses the catch completely. Teammates must practice these plays together many times to perfect the coordination so they happen seamlessly during a game.

The pressure of being a pitcher or catcher may make the job of catching the throw more difficult. For example, with the runner approaching the plate and the game hanging in the balance, the catcher or pitcher covering home plate still must concentrate on catching the ball first. The pitcher or catcher covering home often will set up as a first baseman does, adjusting to where the ball is thrown and either keeping one foot on the plate or reaching down to make a tag. A pitcher may need to catch the throw on the run after a wild pitch and then make a quick tag at the plate. In either case, it is important to remember the basics of catching the ball in an athletic position and then worry about finishing the play.

It would be impossible to prepare for every possible game situation. However it is important to practice catching throws from a variety of angles and speeds. Improving catching ability has little to do with physical size or strength; rather it depends on concentration, anticipation, and in some cases fearlessness. The most reliable defensive players are able to use their visual skills to track throws and anticipate the ball's point of arrival. All players must deal with a certain amount of fear when they see a throw that is off target. Those who can keep their eyes focused on the ball and not shy away allow their natural eye–hand coordination to take over. They see the ball all the way into their gloves.

## PADDLE DRILL

One of the easiest tools to use to practice catching is a hand paddle. A hand paddle is similar to a fielder's glove but doesn't have fingers or a pocket. It can be made out of leather or wood. There are a variety of different ways to use the paddle, but it's easiest to start with a simple catch.

**2.5a-b** Paddle drill.

You and a partner each have a paddle and a tennis ball or safety ball. (A safety ball is the same size and weight as a regular softball but is softer and not as likely to injure someone.) Practice catching the ball with the paddle (figure 2.5a). To catch the ball, you must cover it with the opposite hand, trapping it against the paddle (figure 2.5b). As you become more proficient with this drill, increase the distance between you and your partner, and change the speed of the throw and the location of the catch. Also try bouncing the ball to your partner. First bounce it directly in front of your partner, then off to either side. This drill requires immense concentration. The only way to be successful is to use soft hands and give with the ball as it touches the paddle.

## QUICK CATCH

Another drill that requires a great deal of concentration and incorporates footwork and soft hands is quick catch. Two groups of at least three players each line up approximately 30 feet (9.1 meters) apart (figure 2.6). The lead player in one line throws a ball to the lead player in the other line. As the ball approaches the target, the receiver moves his feet and turns in preparation to catch the ball in front of the throwing-hand shoulder. After catching the ball with soft hands, the receiver throws it back to the first player in the other line as quickly as possible. Both players then move to the ends of their lines. Continue the rotation until someone misses a throw. Repeat the drill.

To add difficulty, use hand paddles and a safety ball.

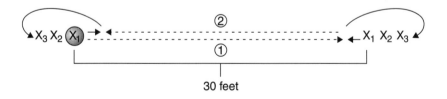

**2.6** **Quick catch.**

## STAR DRILL

This drill requires 15 players. Line up in five groups of three in a star-shaped formation (figure 2.7). One ball is used. To begin the drill, the first player in the line with the ball throws it to the first player in line two groups to the left. The thrower follows the throw and joins the end of that line. The receiver catches the ball by moving her feet and using soft hands. The receiver then quickly throws the ball to the first player in line two groups to the left and follows the throw. The pattern continues around the star until someone drops the ball.

This is the same drill as in chapter 1, except here the focus is on moving the feet to catch the ball and using soft hands.

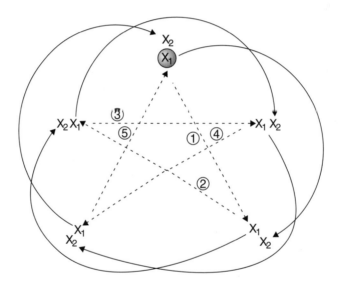

| 2.7 | **Star drill.** |

# Fielding Fly Balls

**A**s home runs have become more prevalent in the game of fastpitch softball, so have the opportunities for outfielders to run down a ball hit into the air and make spectacular catches. Because players are actually trying to hit fly balls, it has made playing the outfield a challenging and very valuable position on any team. An outfielder must possess speed to cover a great deal of the field, a strong arm to throw out speedy base runners, and a fearlessness to make a catch while crashing into a wall or colliding with another player.

Although outfielders get the chance to show their skills by making spectacular catches, they also face the risk of dropping a ball. A fly ball is considered routine when the player sets up properly and the ball falls easily into the glove. But catching a fly ball seems anything but easy when something doesn't go right and the catch isn't made. There could be a million reasons for the miss, including "the sun was in my eyes" excuse. Regardless of the reason, everyone expects a fly ball to be caught; when it isn't others are quick to lay blame. Although catching a fly ball is considered a simple skill, it has many difficult aspects, and it takes a lot of practice.

# Fly Balls

Although we commonly think of catching fly balls as an outfield skill, infielders use these same skills sometimes. The first part of successfully catching a fly ball is to see the ball off the bat as the batter hits it. Judge the angle of the hit, and react to how deep it is.

After you decide to catch the ball, communicate your intention to your teammates. With enough volume so that everyone near the ball can hear you, call the ball with short and clear words at least three times (figure 3.1a). For example, shout, "Mine, mine, mine!"

Anticipate where the ball will fall and move under it, establishing a balanced athletic position with your nonthrowing-side foot slightly in front of the other (figure 3.1b). It is important to be able to move laterally as well as forward and back at the last second in order to adjust to make the catch.

**3.1a**    **Call for the ball as you run to catch it.**

Track the path of the ball with your eyes, and finally raise your glove in time to catch the ball above the throwing-hand shoulder (figure 3.1c). Make sure the glove is high enough above your shoulder to cushion the ball as it lands. To help soften the collision of the ball with the glove, bring your glove hand in toward your body as the ball hits it. This is called giving with the ball. Cover the ball in the glove with your throwing hand to prevent the ball from popping out.

Only after catching the ball should you worry about throwing it. If you have ever seen someone drop a ball because she was trying to throw it too quickly, you know what I mean.

**3.1b** Move under the ball in balanced athletic position.

**3.1c** Move glove to catch the ball.

There are certainly many different ways to catch a fly ball, and often the most fundamentally sound technique isn't the one required to get the job done. In fact, some of the most memorable moments in a game occur when a player must make a diving catch or take a home run away by climbing the fence to pull the ball back in. Watching professional baseball players may give you the impression that making a spectacular catch is more routine than making the typical two-hand catch. The reality is making a great play takes a lot of practice as well as a great deal of athleticism. To make that game-saving catch, you must practice these skills repeatedly. You never know when you might have the opportunity to use them.

**One-Hand Catch**   A simple one-hand catch (figure 3.2) can either be a necessity or an act of laziness that can lose a game. When making a catch on the run, using one hand is preferred since it gives you a longer reach as you extend yourself for the ball. As you run to intercept the ball, continue pumping your arms for maximum speed. Extend your glove arm to meet the ball, and cushion the blow by giving with the ball as it lands in the glove. Secure the ball in the glove with the throwing hand. Establish a proper throwing base by lowering your center of gravity, shortening your steps, and slowing down to change direction.

**3.2**   **One-hand catch.**

**Basket Catch**   One form of the one-hand catch is the basket catch (figure 3.3) because the ball falls into the glove as an apple would fall into a basket. The basket catch is typically used for fly balls that are in front of the player. To make the basket catch, run in to meet the ball, open the glove with the palm up, and point the fingers toward the sky. If your timing is right, the ball will land in the webbing of the glove. Again cushion the landing. The basket catch can be a difficult play, but it may be necessary if you misjudge a fly ball and need to sprint quickly to make the play.

**3.3**   **Basket catch.**

Once in a while, you may have to slide on one knee while making a basket catch. Tuck one foot underneath the knee of the extended leg, similar to sliding into a base, and reach out with the glove hand to make the play (figure 3.4). Sliding allows you to get lower to the ground so you can catch the ball just before it hits the grass.

**3.4**     **One-knee basket catch.**

**Diving Catch**   A great diving catch is a memorable play, but it is a very difficult play and should be practiced often. Whether diving to the side, to the front, or behind you, it is important to be running at full speed just before the catch. After you realize that you won't get to the ball unless you dive for it, lower your center of gravity by bending at the knees, reach out with both arms toward the ball, and watch the ball all the way into your glove (figure 3.5). To help prevent injury, land on your abdomen and keep your chin up so it doesn't smack into the ground. Keep the glove off the ground if possible. The ball might be knocked out of the glove if the glove hits the ground after the ball is caught.

**3.5**   **Diving catch.**

**Backhand Catch**  When running down a ball that is away from your glove side, a backhand catch may be necessary. While sprinting to intercept the ball, extend the glove arm across your body, opening the pocket by rotating your forearm and wrist so that it faces the oncoming ball (figure 3.6). Carefully watch the ball all the way into the glove, then squeeze tightly once the ball is safely in the glove.

**3.6**  Backhand catch.

# Avoiding Collisions

Outfielders catch most fly balls, although it is not uncommon for an infielder to catch a short pop-up or make a catch just behind the infield. The most important thing is that someone catches the ball. Although catching a fly ball may seem to be one of the easier skills in softball, actually an intricate series of events needs to occur for the play to be successful.

Before the ball is even hit, players must understand who is responsible for catching a ball that looks as if it will fall between them. Usually an outfielder has priority over an infielder because the outfielder will have an easier catch as she comes in on the ball. A centerfielder generally has priority over the left and right fielders because of his position in the middle of the outfield. Centerfielders also tend to possess better speed. The shortstop usually is the deepest infielder and should have priority for fly balls on the left side. The second baseman should handle most fly balls on the right side of the infield.

After determining a priority system, agree on a method of communication so that during a difficult play, someone can take charge and call for the ball. Yelling phrases such as "I got it" or "Mine" can prevent collisions between players. It is important to yell the phrase at least three times. If possible, wave your arms to warn others away. Once it is determined who will catch the ball, all other players get in position to fulfill their other responsibilities, such as covering bases, acting as a cutoff for an incoming throw, backing up the player catching the fly ball, or simply telling the player where to throw the ball. This complicated process takes a lot of practice and preparation.

Walk by any schoolyard during the summer months and you will find kids trying to hit fly balls to each other. Often the ball is mishit; few balls actually make it out far enough for any of the defensive players to catch it. To improve your fly ball catching skills, look for simple drills such as ones in which another person throws the ball to you, that require the ball to be hit with a tennis racket, or that use a machine to shoot fly balls.

## SELF-TOSS FOR FLY BALLS

Simply tossing the ball up in the air and catching it can be a great way to practice the art of catching a fly ball. Begin by using a safety ball. Practice catching it without a glove—this will develop the good habits of using two hands and cushioning the ball by giving with it as you catch it. If you get tired of throwing the ball to yourself, try tossing it up onto the roof of your house and catching it as it rolls off, or bounce it off a tall brick wall and practice catching it.

## RUNNING CATCH DRILL

A simple drill to practice catching the ball on the run is to have someone simulate a fly ball by throwing it. Line up a group of players, with a thrower standing slightly to the side. When it is your turn, toss a ball to the thrower and sprint away from her. After going a predetermined distance (the coach will tell you how far to go), the thrower tosses the ball so that you can run it down and make the catch (figure 3.7). Practice calling the ball and setting your feet to throw the ball to the appropriate base after making the catch. If a skilled hitter is available, you can try this drill with the player hitting the ball instead of throwing it.

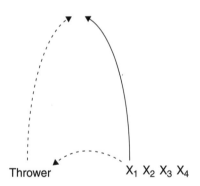

Thrower                     X₁ X₂ X₃ X₄

**3.7**  **Running catch drill.**

## DIVING WIFFLE BALL PROGRESSION

Learning to catch a ball while diving can be a difficult process and usually results in several bruises. A great way to safely practice a diving catch is to use a foam pad or mattress as a landing spot. A coach stands above the pad while you kneel at the end of it. The coach drops a Wiffle ball or a safety ball. Catch the dropped ball by falling forward, keeping your arms and hands off the mat (figure 3.8). Once this skill is mastered, stand up and dive to catch the falling ball. As you build confidence, add some steps before diving. Eventually you will be able to run full speed and dive to catch the ball before it hits the ground. Remember to land on your abdomen, and keep your chin up so it doesn't hit the ground.

**3.8**   **Diving Wiffle ball progression.**

## COMMUNICATION DRILL

You and a partner stand approximately 30 feet (9.1 meters) apart with your backs to a coach. The coach throws the ball into the air so that it will fall between you, then yells, "Ball." When you hear the coach, both of you quickly turn around and look for the ball. When you find the ball and decide to catch it, yell, "Mine, mine, mine!" to let your partner know you will catch it.

# Fielding Ground Balls

In the game of fastpitch softball, several different positions make up the infield. Each of these positions has its own unique assignment requiring different physical and mental qualities. Probably the most important skill for an infielder is the ability to field balls hit along the ground. Because there isn't much distance between an infielder and the batter, it is vital that the infielder possess quick reflexes and stay ready at all times. After fielding the ball, a throw to a base usually must be made. Depending on the speed of the runner, the time an infielder has to throw the ball is usually short, requiring her to make a quick release.

Although both infielders and outfielders field ground balls, the infielder's ability to field ground balls often has more impact on the outcome of the game. The mental aspect of playing the infield is one of the most crucial skills. An infielder will face many different plays and situations and must be able to anticipate what will happen next. Before a pitch is thrown, all infielders should know what to do if the ball comes their way and where the play will be made if the ball goes to someone else. As most infielders will tell you, getting dirty is part of the job. Taking pride in the ability to dive, field a ground ball, and quickly throw out a runner is the trademark of a successful infielder.

# Fielding Ground Balls

It is impossible to field every ground ball the same way, but the basic technique can be used most of the time. Start in a basic athletic position, feet slightly wider than shoulders. Bend forward at the knees and waist. Extend your arms down and away from you, and bend at the knees until you can touch the ground. Your hands should end up about four to six inches (10 to 15 centimeters) in front of your feet (figure 4.1a). Feel your weight on the balls of your feet, almost as if you were falling forward.

Once your feet feel set, place your fielding glove flat on the ground, with the pocket turned up and the fingers pointing toward the ball. Track the ball from the bat with your eyes, and field the ground ball directly between your feet. Keep your chin tucked down to your chest to help your eyes stay focused on the ball (figure 4.1b). As the ball rolls into the glove, cover the ball with your throwing hand to keep it secure. Cradle the ball, pulling it to your abdomen (figure 4.1c).

**4.1a** Athletic position for fielding a ground ball.

**4.1b** Fielding glove flat on ground, eyes on ball.

Keep your feet and body still as you field the ground ball. You will develop soft hands and become a consistent fielder. Resist the tendency to surround the sides of the ball with your hands. If your timing is not perfect, the ball could slip between your hands, resulting in an error. If your glove is already on the ground, it will block the ball from getting past.

Only after you secure the ball to your abdomen should you begin the throwing process. Find the proper grip on the ball, take a small gather step for balance (figure 4.1d), line up to the target, and throw the ball. Depending on the situation, you may not need to throw the ball at all. You may need to simply tag a base or a runner. Anticipate the possible plays before the pitch so you can react quickly when the time comes. A good infielder will always be ready to make the play whether the ball is hit to her or not.

**4.1d** Take a gather step.

**4.1c** Cradle ball to abdomen.

Depending on the climate in which you live, practicing ground balls on dirt may or may not be possible. If you live in a cold or wet climate, a lot of practice time will be spent indoors, making it difficult to simulate grounders on dirt. A dirt infield can cause various bounces and tricky hops that you will need to anticipate. Rarely will an easy ground ball be hit directly to you. Practice these and other difficult fielding skills to prepare for playing in a game.

**Charging the Ball**   One of the secrets to being a good infielder is charging the ball. You can save valuable time by running up on the ball to field it. That time is critical when trying to throw out a quick runner. Reacting to the speed of the ball is crucial since you also will need to charge ground balls that aren't hit very hard. Once you decide to charge the ball, quickly move your feet, then make sure you are in proper athletic position to field the ball (figure 4.2). It doesn't do any good to charge the ball if you are unable to set up before the ball arrives.

**4.2**   **Charging a ground ball.**

**Short Hop**   A short hop, a ground ball that bounces just in front of you, can be a difficult ball to field cleanly. It is hard to judge how the ball will bounce because of its spin, but by using soft hands you can adjust to different hops quite easily. Stay in good athletic position, and watch the ball all the way into the glove (figure 4.3). Depending on the speed of the ball, you may need to charge to get into proper position. With your chin down and hands out in front, anticipate the ball's contact point with the ground, and try to match how the ball will bounce with your glove. After correctly calculating the hop, give with the ball into your abdomen, cushion it, and prepare for the throw. If you miscalculate the hop, you should still be able to field the ground ball if you set up properly. Your body should be in position to block the ball even if you don't get your glove on it. By being in front of the ball, even if you miscalculate the hop, you are likely to keep the ball in front and still have a play.

**4.3**   **Fielding a short hop.**

**Backhand**   A backhand play is a last resort if the ball is hit so hard
you don't have time to move into proper fielding position. You don't
have much time to react, so you must quickly decide on the backhand
play. To get into proper position, use a crossover step in which your
glove-side foot crosses in front of your body (figure 4.4a). Stay low
to the ground during the crossover step by keeping both knees bent;
sometimes the knee on the throwing-hand side may need to rest on
the ground. Make the backhand play by reaching across your body,
with the glove turned to field the ball (figure 4.4b). Be sure the glove
is out in front of your body. As the ball reaches the glove, cushion
the catch by giving with the ball until it is secure. It will take a little
more time to regain your footwork to make a good throw.

## Backhand Play

4.4a   **Take a crossover step to get into
position.**

4.4b   **Reach across your body, with glove
turned to field the ball.**

**Diving Stop**  Making a great diving play is usually more about attitude than great athleticism. Diving plays are possible only if you are willing to throw your body on the ground and risk getting injured or, more likely, a little dusty. After determining that you cannot stop the ball unless you dive, begin to angle your body toward the anticipated point of the dive. Move at an angle toward the outfield to give yourself some additional time to field the ground ball. Stay low to the ground as you move. At the last possible second, dive to intercept the ball (figure 4.5). Land on your abdomen, with your glove arm extended and the pocket of the glove open to the ball. Sometimes it is impossible to field the ball cleanly into the glove, but you may be able to smother it into the ground, preventing it from reaching the outfield. On a diving play, your primary goal is to stop the ball. Rarely will you have enough time to get up and make a throw to a base for an out.

**4.5**   **Diving stop.**

# Fielding Outfield Grounders

So far in this chapter, we have mostly talked about infield ground ball techniques, and rightly so, since the majority of ground balls are in the infield. Infielders usually have little time to react and need to make a play as quickly as possible. With a runner sprinting down the line, the pressure to cleanly field the ball and quickly make a throw is great. For outfielders, ground balls are also part of the game, but outfield players are more concerned with stopping the ball and making an accurate throw back to the infield.

As an outfielder, you will use three types of ground ball techniques, depending on the game situation. First, if no one is on base, you should use the one-knee technique in which you put one knee on the ground and create a wall to stop the ball. Your primary goal with this technique is to keep the ball in front and prevent the runner from advancing. If the base runner is exceptionally fast, the ball is hit to either side, or the batter gets a hit with a runner on first base, you should use an infield technique. Assume a solid athletic position to keep the ball in front, and make a quick throw to the proper base. The infield technique is a little faster than the one-knee technique, and you will have a better chance to keep the runners from advancing.

The final outfield fielding technique, called a do or die, is used when the batter gets a hit with a runner on second base. You must quickly field the ground ball and make a strong throw all the way to home plate to stop the runner. Begin by charging the ball as quickly as possible to cut down the distance for the throw and also to save time. Then field the ball on the run by scooping it up with the glove, transfer it to the throwing hand, and in the same motion throw the ball to home plate. This is a riskier play since it would be easy for the ground ball to take a funny hop and get past you, but because your concern is the runner heading for home, it is the best option in this situation.

Practice and preparation will help you develop confidence as a fielder. These drills will improve confidence in your abilities. They also are designed to be safe and prepare you for live game situations.

## BARE HANDED

This drill is designed to teach you how to field the ball with your hands rather than a glove. Use a safety ball so you won't hurt your hands. Stand about 7 to 10 feet (2.1 to 3.0 meters) away from a partner and face each other. Begin with your partner as the tosser and you as the fielder. The tosser rolls the ball directly at you. Practice fielding the ball with your hands under and on top of the ball. Give with the ball into your abdomen, then backhand the ball to your partner. Work on following the ball into your hands with your eyes, and keep a good fielding position the entire time. Staying in correct fielding position will develop leg strength and endurance. Do 10 to 15 repetitions and then switch roles. After each of you complete the first set, your partner rolls the ball to one side and then the other, making you move your feet to get in front of the ball. Be sure to use the same good fielding technique.

## ONE HOPPERS

Once again stand facing your partner about 10 feet (3.0 meters) away from each other. You will need to practice on a smooth, solid surface so the ball will bounce consistently and allow you to correctly anticipate the hop. Your partner tosses a safety ball so that it bounces directly in front of you, simulating a short hop. At first use only your bare hands to field the ball; eventually you can try this drill with a paddle or even a fielder's glove. Keep your feet still, and stay in a good athletic position. Give with the ball into your abdomen, concentrating on keeping your head down. After 10 to 15 repetitions, switch roles with your partner. After you are used to the drill, have your partner toss the ball to one side then the other, and field the ball with a fielder's glove.

## FIELDING ON KNEES

Another drill that can help you develop soft hands and improve your ability to see the ball into the glove is fielding ground balls from a kneeling position. Use a safety ball to limit the risk of injury. Kneel on a firm surface so you will see consistent ground balls. Have a coach hit ground balls directly at you, first slowly and then faster as you gain confidence and skill. Practice fielding the ball out in front and using soft hands to give with the ball into your abdomen.

## DIVING PROGRESSION

Learning to dive and stop a ground ball is an important skill for an infielder. Use a safety ball and a padded mat. Begin on your knees. A partner or coach rolls the ball to either side, out of your reach unless you sprawl on the ground. Keep your eye on the ball, and watch it all the way into your glove. Once you feel comfortable with this skill, stand and dive to the ground to field the ball (figure 4.6). Finally put it all together by running and diving to stop the ball.

**4.6** Diving progression.

# Playing Catcher

One of the most difficult positions to play in the game of softball is catcher. A catcher must possess a great deal of skill, toughness, and leadership ability. Throwing out a runner trying to steal second or picking off a would-be base stealer at first requires great arm strength as well as a quick release. Because a catcher is involved in every pitch during a game, she must be aware of each situation and be able to direct the rest of the team. It could be telling the pitcher to throw a certain pitch, communicating with a cutoff, or encouraging a teammate to succeed. On throws to home plate, the catcher communicates with the cutoff—the infielder positioned between the catcher and the outfielder. The catcher directs the cutoff to catch the ball and throw it home or to another base.

# Behind the Plate

As a catcher, you will spend a majority of the game in a squatting position behind the plate, anticipating the arrival of the ball from the pitcher. Finding a comfortable position is critical. Start with your feet about shoulder-width apart; as you lower yourself into position, be sure to maintain good balance. Extend your mitt toward the pitcher, and keep the throwing hand hidden behind your knee to protect against unnecessary broken or jammed fingers (figure 5.1a). Besides throwing the ball, the one time you need to keep your hand free is when giving the pitcher signals. Usually, signals are given by flashing a predetermined number of fingers, being careful not to allow the opposing team to see them. To prevent the other team from seeing the signals, keep your fingers tight to your body, and use your legs to block the other team's view.

Once the pitcher is ready to begin her motion, giving her a good target to throw at is vital. Sometimes moving to the inside or outside of the plate while anticipating the pitch location can be helpful. However, be careful not to give away the location of the pitch to the other team too soon. One of the most difficult aspects of playing catcher is concentrating on the ball while a hitter swings at it. You don't know whether the batter will swing and miss, make good contact, or foul the ball off your face mask or some other body part. It takes a tremendous amount of concentration and toughness to sit perfectly still, waiting for the ball to arrive, while someone swings a metal club a few inches from your head.

As the ball arrives, framing it into the strike zone is a skill that any pitcher would love to see in his catcher. To make the borderline pitch a strike, catch the outside of the ball and move it in toward the plate by curling your wrist. For those balls that bounce in the dirt, blocking rather than catching them becomes the priority. When the ball bounces in the dirt, it is no longer a matter of the umpire calling it a strike but of keeping it from going all the way to the backstop. Keep the ball centered within your body, kick back your feet, and let your knees land where your feet were (figure 5.1b). As the ball skips toward you, lean forward and tuck your chin, blocking the ball with your chest protector. Remember, the goal is to keep the ball in front of you and prevent the runners from easily advancing a base.

As a catcher, a strong, accurate throwing arm is certainly a prerequisite, although a quick release can make up for some lack of arm strength. The longest throw you should have to make is down to second base on a steal attempt. Some catchers like to release this throw while still on their knees, but this is usually a risky play, and few have the ability to pull it off. Most of the time, use the fundamental throwing technique with a small step toward the base, using your body turn to create power in the throw. The only real difference is creating a quicker release. When throwing down to first or third base in a pickoff situation, you may want to try to turn more quickly by rotating your body with a two-foot jump. Remember to stay in a good athletic position, always ready to react to a runner's move. Although a quick release is important, so is a good accurate throw with proper spin on the ball.

**5.1a**　**Squatting position.**

**5.1b**　**Blocking.**

The catcher is involved in virtually every play during a game and must be prepared to make a play on every pitch. Continually communicate with the coach and discuss strategy between innings. Rarely does something happen on the field that doesn't involve the catcher in one way or another.

**Intentional Walks**   When four balls are thrown during an at-bat, the batter advances to first base on a "walk." Some coaches will use the walk as a tool to avoid pitching to a good hitter. An intentional walk is usually called for when first base is unoccupied and a good hitter is up to bat. It not only keeps the good hitter from driving in runs but also adds another force-out opportunity to get out of an inning—the defense can get an out by just touching a base, rather than having to tag a runner. As the catcher, you would typically stand up and hold out your hand to signify to the pitcher what is happening, and also to give her a target for the intentional ball (figure 5.2). Stay in the catcher's box until the pitch is released, then move out to catch the ball. If runners are on base, make sure they know you are paying attention to them. Look directly at them each time you catch the ball, and keep an infielder close to the base in case you need to throw her way.

**5.2**   **Calling an intentional ball.**

**Passed Balls and Wild Pitches**   Occasionally, a pitcher will make a wild throw that gets by you to the backstop, or a ball that should have been caught bounces away. Many catchers will go into a panic while chasing down the ball, then wildly make a throw, trying to get an advancing runner. It is important to stay calm and realize the potential of making a play somewhere is limited, and it may be better to just pick up the ball and get ready for the next pitch. If a runner is heading home on the play and there is a chance of getting her out, quickly get to the ball and put your body in position to make a toss at the same time. As you approach the ball, slide on your knees so that you are turned sideways and can pick up the ball and make the throw to the pitcher covering home plate in the same motion. Keep the throw low to the ground so it can easily be caught for a quick tag.

**Plays at the Plate**   One of the more dramatic plays in the game of softball is throwing a runner out at home plate to prevent a score. Always anticipate the potential play well before it occurs. If it is a force out, keep only one foot on the plate and stretch toward the ball. Once you catch the ball, get out of the way of the sliding runner to prevent any injuries or other base runners from advancing. On a tag play, straddle the plate, allowing the runner room to safely slide if he beats the throw home (figure 5.3). If you catch the ball before the runner can get there, drop your left knee down to the ground and apply the tag, preventing him from scoring. Always be prepared for a collision with the runner, whether intentional or not, by staying in a good athletic position and being ready to receive a blow.

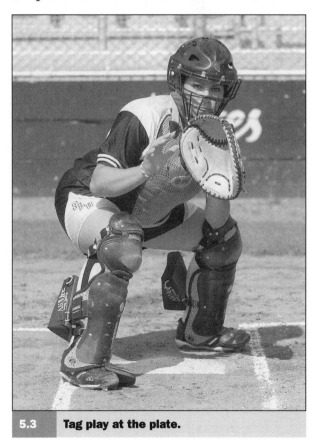

**5.3**   **Tag play at the plate.**

**Fielding Bunts**   When a hitter sees the infielders playing a good distance away, she may try to bunt the ball. A bunt is a softly hit ball that doesn't travel very far from home plate and makes the infielders run up to field it. Most bunts should be covered by the third baseman, but if the ball is just in front of the plate you should make the play. After the ball has been bunted, quickly determine who has the best chance of fielding the ball, and if it is you, let everyone else know your intentions. Get your body turned in preparation for a throw even before picking up the ball. Bend your knees and quickly scoop up the ball with both hands, then throw to the appropriate base. If additional runners are on, get back to home plate to prepare for a play.

**Fielding Pop-Ups**   A "pop-up"—when the batter hits the ball straight up in the air—can be a tough play. As a catcher, handling

a pop-up can be difficult because of the spin on the ball and also the gear you're wearing. Once you recognize the play is yours to make, take off your catcher's mask and toss it far enough away so that you won't trip on it, but be careful not to hit an umpire or another player. Because of the spin on the ball when it goes straight up, the ball will usually come back toward the playing field. If it is high enough in the air, take the time to turn around and face the backstop for an easier play (figure 5.4). Stay in a good athletic position, and let everyone know you will be catching the ball. Give with the ball as it hits your mitt, and prepare to make a throw to another base if possible.

**5.4**   **Fielding a pop-up.**

**Cutoffs**  When a ball is hit past an outfielder, it is generally going to require a second throw to get to the catcher. It is your responsibility to line up the cutoff person in the correct spot and also tell her whether to cut it off and which base to throw to. Anticipate the situation before it occurs, and remind the potential cutoff of her responsibilities. As the play happens, give loud and clear instructions to the players. Keep the entire field in your view, and watch the timing of the play and where the runners are. If there is a better chance of getting an out at another base, yell this to the cutoff so she can make that throw instead.

**Backing Up**  In addition to all of your other catching responsibilities, it is important to back up throws to first base. If a throw is coming from the shortstop or second baseman toward first and no other runners are on base, follow the runner down the line. If a bad throw gets by the first baseman, you can prevent the runner from getting into scoring position by backing up the play. Stay well into foul territory, and anticipate the angle of the throw before it happens. By staying outside the foul lines, you create room between you and the player covering the base, which can allow you to react to any poor throws.

*Take it to the field*

# Coach on the Field

If there were such a thing as a coach on the field, the catcher would be the most likely candidate. You are in position to view the entire field and are involved with every pitch, sometimes more than once. In one ear, a coach is shouting instructions to you for each situation; in the other, you hear a coach trying to find out why the umpire didn't call the pitch a strike. In between innings, getting a chance to rest is rarely an option. The coach wants to establish strategy, find out what is working and what isn't, and then someone screams that it's your turn to hit.

Even before the game starts your work as a catcher is important. Warming up a pitcher can be an experience in and of itself. Some pitchers prefer to warm up slowly, and others will need only a few short minutes. As the catcher, you need to know the wants and needs of each of your pitchers and how much time each needs before a game. You must also be half psychologist and know when to comfort and certainly motivate a pitcher when things aren't going well. Building a pitcher's confidence begins before the game and requires a great amount of skill.

*(continued)*

## Coach on the Field, *continued*

As the game begins, it is your responsibility to either call each pitch or relay the signal from the coach. Being able to anticipate the strengths and weaknesses of the hitter and matching them with what the pitcher can throw is a tremendous art. You need to think as the coach does, yet make sure the pitcher has confidence in that pitch for a given situation. Usually, analyzing the hitter's stance and swing can give you some hints as to any weaknesses, but the best tool is recall of his previous at-bat—which pitch was thrown and what was the result.

When runners get on base, you are responsible for relaying the appropriate play for that situation. Everyone on the field looks to the catcher to give guidance and provide the answers during crucial moments in the game. Speak loudly and with confidence. Get players' attention by calling out their names and pointing at them when you give specific instructions; be sure they acknowledge the message.

If a pitcher is having a difficult time during the game, it is up to the catcher to find the right thing to say and how to say it. Sometimes you may need to lighten the mood by making a joke, and at other times it may be necessary to be firm with the pitcher. In either case, the team is relying on you to find a way to improve the pitcher's performance. You must also let a coach know when a pitcher is getting tired and can't get the job done any longer. It is a difficult responsibility to maintain trust and friendship with a teammate, yet let the coach know what is best for the team.

*Give it a go*

It is often difficult for a catcher to work on skills during practice. If you're not hitting with the rest of the team, your primary responsibility is catching a pitcher. Many days can go by without a chance to work on your skills, but when it counts you still need to perform. Take time to hone your skills with these drills, which may mean asking a coach to come early or stay late for a practice.

## BLOCKING DRILLS

One of the most important skills a catcher must master is the ability to block a ball from going to the backstop. Blocking well takes courage, agility, and good reactions. Ask a coach or another player to simulate a pitch in the dirt by gently tossing balls in front of you. If you are just a beginner, use Wiffle balls or safety balls to prevent injury and to build your confidence. As you become more skilled, have the balls come more quickly and also to either side.

## REAR TOSS

Rear toss is a good reaction drill for the catcher. Have a person stand behind you and toss balls over your shoulder to simulate a bunt. Practice proper footwork and picking up the ball. Finish the play by throwing to an appropriate base, or just simulate the throw. Good footwork should put your body in position to throw without any additional movement. When picking up a ball that is not moving, push it into the ground to help get the grip more easily.

## THREE BALL DRILL

Work on quickness and proper foot positioning with this drill. Place three balls a couple feet apart, beginning just outside home plate down the third base line (figure 5.5). Start in the proper catching

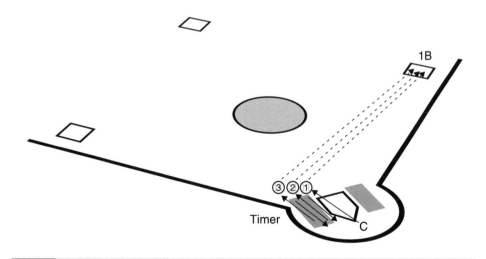

**5.5** **Three ball drill.**

position behind home plate. Ask an assistant to start timing the drill when you move toward the first ball. Quickly pick up the first ball using proper footwork and throw to the target (for example, an infielder), then quickly return to and touch home plate. After touching the plate, sprint to the next ball and throw to the target. Sprint back to home plate, then quickly return to the final ball and make the throw. When the final ball reaches the target, the assistant should stop the timer and record the time. You can compare times between trials, between different days, or with another player.

## POP-UP DRILL

Ask an assistant to simulate pop-ups by hitting balls straight into the air with a racquetball or tennis racket. It is much easier to use a racket than a bat to hit the ball straight up. As you become more proficient at catching the pop-ups, have the assistant make the catches more difficult by hitting the balls higher and farther away. If you have access to a motorized pitching machine, you can use the same drill with greater precision.

# Pitching

**A** fastpitch pitcher is one of the most prominent players on the field. The pitcher is the only player who handles the ball on every play of the game. She also controls the pace of the game. The pitcher's attitude can influence the mentality of the entire team; other players often look to the pitcher for inspiration and leadership.

Becoming a great pitcher requires hours of year-round practice. At times when other players may not be thinking of softball at all, the dedicated pitcher is continually working on new pitches and refining old ones.

Although certain physical characteristics can benefit a pitcher, the greatest attributes are mental composure and toughness. A tall pitcher with long legs and arms can hold a physical advantage over a smaller player, but the pitcher's mental ability will make the greatest difference during a game.

# Pitch It!

Some rules allow the pitcher to place only one foot on the pitching plate, while others require that both feet stay in contact with the plate as the pitcher takes the signal and begins the pitching motion. For a right-handed pitcher, the right foot is forward, with the toes slightly off the front of the pitching plate. The left foot can be toward the back of the circle or even in the dirt, with just the toes touching the back of the plate.

When you receive the signal, your hands should be apart (figure 6.1a). The ball can be in either your glove or your pitching hand. Before beginning the pitching motion, establish a line of power that extends from your front foot to the point of home plate. Simply visualize this line, and use it as a reference during the pitch.

Begin the pitching motion with your hands together and the ball in the glove. Move your arms forward up the center of your body, following the line of power toward home plate (figure 6.1b). At the same time, transfer your weight to the balls of your feet and begin

**6.1a** Hands apart to receive signal.

**6.1b** Arms move forward, hands together, ball in glove.

to push forward off your feet. As your arms rise to your shoulders, all of your weight goes on your pitching-hand foot (the right foot for a right-handed pitcher). At this point, pivot onto your power line by putting your weight on your big toe and driving into the dirt. Simultaneously drive your opposite knee up and forward so that the foot lands on the power line (figure 6.1c). You should be balanced on the balls of your feet, with your body weight on the line of power, knees bent and shoulders over knees.

Throughout the pitching motion, your arm should make a perfect circle in front of your body. To make a perfect circle, bring your pitching arm directly in front, passing the arm next to your ear. As you pivot, let your arm drop directly down to the point of releasing the ball (figure 6.1d). After the release, bring it up again until your fingers come over your shoulder as you complete the pivot. If you were holding a piece of chalk next to a blackboard, you could draw this perfect circle while performing the pitching motion.

**6.1c**  **Pivot onto the power line.**

**6.1d**  **Bring arm down to release point.**

Spin on the ball makes it move in different directions as the seams catch the air. Most pitchers throw five basic pitches: fastball, change-up, drop ball, rise ball, and curveball. Most pitchers can throw a drop ball since gravity helps the pitcher make the ball move down, and the pitch doesn't require a lot of speed. However a rise ball works against gravity, so you must throw it with a great deal of velocity.

**Follow Through**  Follow through after releasing the ball (figure 6.2). Follow through with your legs, beginning at the point at which you released the ball. After the release, pivot your front toe and push forward. At the same time, push your back leg forward by driving toward the front knee. Stay on the line of power. Follow through with your arm by keeping the circle going, finishing with your elbow at shoulder height and your fingers over your shoulder. Use your arm as a lever. Strive to keep your arm as long as possible throughout the circle and the pitching motion.

**6.2**    **Follow through.**

**Fastball**  The grip is the critical starting point, and it varies for each pitch. The fastball uses the same grip (figure 6.3) as throwing the ball overhand. Be sure the pads of your fingers lie on the seams, with the middle finger centered on the ball. If your fingers rest off to one side, the ball will tend to spin sideways, causing inconsistency with the fastball.

Developing wrist snap is one of the most important aspects when throwing a fastball. The more snap you can get behind the ball, the more spin it will have and the faster it will go. To maximize wrist snap, cock your wrist back and snap it straight through as quickly as possible, letting the ball roll off your fingers at release. The ball should spin as if you had made an overhand throw. The release point for the fastball is just inside the front leg, when your body is still in the pivot (figure 6.4).

**6.3**  Grip for the fastball.

**6.4**  Release point for the fastball.

**59**

**Change-Up**   Although a change-up does not necessarily move a lot on its way to home plate, it does have a significantly different speed than the fastball. The goal is to make the change-up go slower than the fastball but keep the same pitching motion so the batter can't adjust to the speed of the pitch.

To make the ball go slower and to reduce its spin, you need to change your grip. A general rule of thumb is that the more skin on the ball, the slower the ball will go. To grip the ball for a change-up, place it in your palm and wrap your fingers around it, keeping the ball in contact with the heel of your hand (figure 6.5).

The motion needs to be the same as for a fastball. The only difference is how the ball is released. Instead of snapping your wrist, as with a fastball, keep your wrist snap to a minimum, and push the ball toward the plate. Because the ball will be going slower, release it slightly later than you would a fastball (figure 6.6).

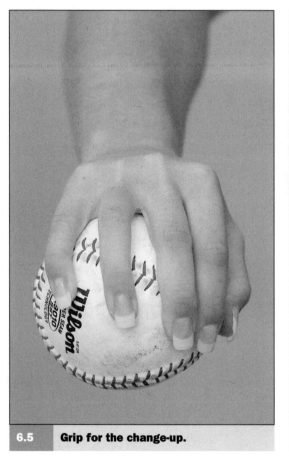

**6.5**   Grip for the change-up.

**6.6**   Release point for the change-up.

**Drop Ball**   The drop ball should do exactly what the name implies—drop toward the ground. The two primary ways to throw the drop ball are the turnover drop and the peel drop. In both cases, it is important to create a great deal of topspin on the ball so it catches the air and moves down.

With a peel drop, hold the ball as you would a fastball except put your middle three fingers together so they are touching (figure 6.7). Keep your fingertips on the seams so that when you release the ball you can create a lot of spin by pulling against the seams. Shorten your stride slightly, and make sure you are in good pivot position at release. To release the ball, bend your elbow and snap the ball off your fingertips, pulling in a backward motion to add additional spin (figure 6.8). The follow-through will be much shorter than with a regular fastball.

**6.7**   Grip for the peel drop ball.

**6.8**   Release point for the peel drop ball.

A turnover drop achieves the same spin on the ball as a peel drop, but it creates a little more strain on the elbow and shoulder because of the turn of the elbow. Again use a slightly shorter stride to throw the turnover drop. Grip the ball with the outside of your index finger running along a seam (figure 6.9). As you get ready to release the ball, bend your elbow so that the ball is slightly away from your body. Cock your wrist into a position in which the palm of your hand is toward the catcher (figure 6.10). As you release the ball, create topspin by using your wrist and elbow to turn the ball over. Follow through in a downward motion, slightly across your body.

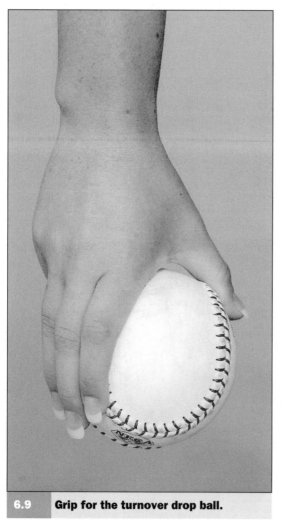

**6.9**   **Grip for the turnover drop ball.**

**6.10**   **Release point for the turnover drop ball.**

**Rise Ball**   To make a rise ball effective, you must be able to throw the ball with a lot of velocity to fight the effects of gravity. Grip the ball with the inside of your index finger, making contact with the seam along its entire length (figure 6.11). Although there are many different ways to grip the ball with the rest of the fingers, depending on individual preference, the goal with any grip is to create backspin on the ball. The rise ball requires a longer stride than normal, and you must bend your back knee to create an upward angle with your hips and shoulders.

As you are about to release the ball, keep your weight back on your rear leg, almost as if you were leaning backward. Cock your wrist and keep your arm long and close to your body. As you release the ball, forcefully turn your wrist to create backspin on the ball, keeping your elbow close to your body (figure 6.12). This motion is similar to opening a doorknob but obviously much more forceful. The follow-through is slightly away from your body.

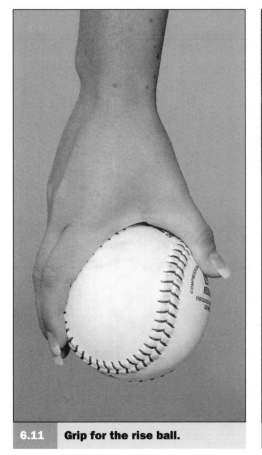

6.11   **Grip for the rise ball.**

6.12   **Release point for the rise ball.**

**63**

**Curveball**   A curveball from a right-handed pitcher will tend to move away from a right-handed hitter. It can be a tremendously difficult pitch to hit. In the previous pitches, the line of force kept the arm in a perfect circle. For an effective curveball, you want to step across the line of force and pull the ball across your body.

The grip for a curveball is similar to the grip for a drop ball, with the seams of the ball on the outside of your finger (figure 6.13). As you stride, step across the line of force by about a foot to create a new angle of delivery. At this point, if you were to let the ball go straight it would head right for the hitter. As you are about to release the ball, pull it across your body to put a sideways spin on the ball (figure 6.14). Keep your elbow in tight to your body until after the ball is released, then let it follow through away from your body. Usually a little downward spin can make the curveball an even more difficult pitch to hit.

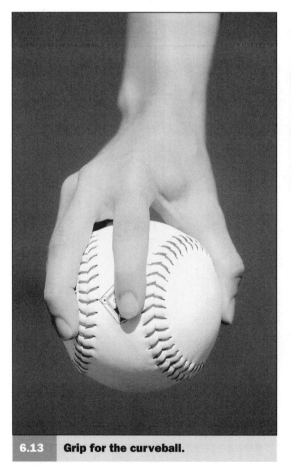

**6.13**   Grip for the curveball.

**6.14**   Release point for the curveball.

# Committing to the Game

Developing a proper mentality for stepping into the pitching circle is an important part of any pitcher's training. Few athletic endeavors require the mental toughness and ability to stay calm and focused during critical situations as much as pitching in fastpitch softball. Although a team is composed of many players, the pitcher is the one everyone relies on for the success of the team. Because this single player can dominate the game, the rest of the team often looks to the pitcher for inspiration, hope, and success.

Before you can enjoy success as a pitcher, you must commit to the game. You must enjoy the attention that comes from playing the position. Good or bad, others will always judge your performance and that of the team based on what you do in the pitcher's circle. It takes commitment to develop and refine your skill all year round. When other players take time off or do other activities, a pitcher's conditioning and practice time rarely even slows down. If you choose to take extended time off from the game, the feel of each pitch and your fitness will greatly diminish. Working into shape and regaining the feel of playing the game are often more work than maintaining conditioning and skill during the off-season.

In preparation for starting a game, you also must learn about the opposing team and its strengths and weaknesses. The catcher is a critical link in your success, and it starts with warming up for a game and recognizing what pitches are working well and why. A good catcher can help you find the answers to why one pitch worked once and then didn't the next time. By building a strong, trusting relationship with your catcher, you will have a partner to discuss situations and strategy before, during, and after a game.

When you enter the circle, you will have a plan for each situation. However, things don't always go as planned. An umpire may not give you the strike zone you expected, hitters may be better than anticipated, or teammates may make fielding errors. Regardless of the adversity, it is up to you to deal with every situation and find a way to succeed. Stay ahead of the count to make the hitter more anxious. Defensive players enjoy playing with a pitcher who keeps the game moving along by throwing strikes. If you try to be perfect and end up walking a lot of hitters or get behind in the count, you give the hitter extra confidence and your teammates become anxious.

Dealing with pressure takes a combination of physical ability and mental toughness. By preparing yourself for difficult situations in practice and perfecting your physical skills, you can handle any situation that may arise in a game.

Using drills to practice pitching skills is common, but concentrating and learning from these drills is the difficult part. Just as a lot of students think they will be doctors when they enroll in college, many young softball players think they will be great pitchers. Unfortunately it is not that easy. Developing the skills and mental toughness required is a long and difficult road.

## WRIST SNAP

Learning how to use wrist snap to make the ball spin properly is an important skill for any pitcher. For a fastball spin, tape a line down the middle of the ball so you can see if it is spinning correctly. Begin by placing your middle finger on the taped line. Hold your upper arm tight to your body, and toss the ball into the air with a wrist snap. As you become more proficient, see how high you can throw the ball by using just the wrist snap to send the ball upward.

## SIDEWAYS RELEASE

The next development stage in pitching is to use the wrist snap drill while standing in the pivot position. Stand sideways to the target in good athletic position. Practice raising the ball above your head, cocking your wrist, then letting your arm fall and snapping the ball toward a target. With practice, you can make the ball spin straight and hit the target on a regular basis. Progress in this drill by throwing the ball harder or placing small dots on the wall as miniature targets.

## FRONT TO PIVOT

Begin by facing the target, whether a catcher or a brick wall, and simulate a pitch by stepping forward and releasing the ball as for the sideways release drill. Stay in the pivot position after release, and monitor the spin and location of the pitch. Concentrate on maintaining the perfect circle and using the line of force to keep track of the ball's path to the target. You can advance this drill by throwing the ball harder or moving the target, but maintain a good athletic pivot position following release. This is a good warm-up drill for pitchers at any level and will help you find the release point of various pitches and target locations.

## PITCHING FROM ONE KNEE

Arm strength and speed are crucial tools for a pitcher. If you are right handed, kneel on your right knee, with your left knee bent at 90 degrees. Position yourself sideways to the target. Make a circular motion with the ball, following the line of force, and release the ball from the kneeling position. If you have difficulty with the perfect circle, perform this drill close to a wall so your arm will stay true to the line of force.

## BALL SPINS

Another good warm-up drill for all pitchers is to stand in the sideways release position and practice various ball spins. Alternate drop ball, rise ball, and curveball spins, creating muscle memory for each pitch. Place electrical tape around the center of the ball so you can follow the spin of each pitch and evaluate its success.

## FOOTBALL TOSS

A good drill for practicing the rise ball is the football toss. Find a small to medium football that fits your hand comfortably. Practice the wrist snap drill. Stand still and just use your wrist to make the ball spin true and down the line of force. Feel the ball come off your hand. You can use the football for the sideways release drill, for pitching from one knee, or even to go through a full pitching motion.

# Hitting

**H**itting has been called one of the most difficult skills in all of sport. If you are successful a third of the time, you would be considered very talented, one of the best in the game. A hall of fame baseball player might have been successful only three out of ten times at bat yet is memorialized for his achievement. By these numbers, it is clear that hitting is a difficult skill to master, and to a great degree, success depends on natural talent. Eye–hand coordination, visual acuity, hand speed, and overall muscular strength are a few of the characteristics a good hitter possesses. However, with practice, determination, and mental training, anyone can become a better hitter, regardless of her natural abilities. By working on the fundamentals of hitting, you develop better balance and bat speed, as well as improve your ability to see the ball.

Although many tools, machines, and aids are available to help a player become a better hitter, it all begins with the bat. Finding a bat that fits you is never an easy task. There isn't a good formula to determine the proper length and weight of a bat, so it is important to test a variety of them. In general, you should look for the heaviest bat you can swing while maintaining the most bat speed. Picking the length of a bat depends on your height and also your ability to keep maximum bat speed through the hitting zone.

# Connecting With the Ball

Good hitting begins with a proper stance. Creating balance is crucial throughout your swing. Begin with your feet slightly wider than your shoulders. If you have extremely long legs, then widen your feet a little. A good rule of thumb is to position your feet as if you were fielding a ground ball. To have good balance, you must bend forward slightly at the waist and allow your knees to also bend slightly.

In the stance, the front elbow is bent at 90 degrees, in the shape of an L, and the rear elbow resembles a V pointing toward the ground (figure 7.1a). Many coaches encourage players to keep their back elbow up in the stance. This can lead to several problems in the swing, including tightness through the shoulder area. By staying relaxed, your hands will move more quickly, resulting in greater bat speed. In addition, if you squeeze the bat too tightly, the swing slows down and bat control is diminished. Your bat should be held comfortably in the fingers, with the knuckles you would use to knock on a door lined up to help with the wrist snap.

Being able to time your swing with the arrival of the ball is the next obstacle to overcome as a hitter. Usually, a good point of reference

**7.1a** **Good position for hitting the ball.**

**7.1b** **Pivot.**

is to start with a short stride as the pitcher releases the ball. If you overstride, too much weight will shift onto the front foot, causing your eyes to move forward and down, making it more difficult to see the ball. A good analogy for the stride is to imagine you are stepping onto a frozen pond, checking to see how strong it is. If you put too much weight on that first step, you may break through the ice.

Now that the swing has started, you have about two-tenths of a second to decide whether the pitch is a ball or a strike. If it is a strike, then you have about another two-tenths of a second to make that perfect swing and connect with the ball. Power in the swing begins by pivoting the back foot, allowing the knee and hip to turn easily. As you rotate the hips, keep your hands back in the launching position as long as possible (figure 7.1b). This creates some torque in the body, resulting in greater bat speed. At the final possible moment, release your hands toward the ball, snapping your wrists to make contact (figure 7.1c). Follow through with the bat above your shoulder, maintaining balance throughout the swing (figure 7.1d).

**7.1c** **Snap wrists as hands release toward ball.**

**7.1d** **Follow through.**

Your physical size and strength determine how much power the swing generates, and ultimately how far the ball travels. However, practicing the proper fundamentals can make anyone a better hitter. Learning to hit the ball to the opposite field, executing a hit and run when called on, or scoring a runner from third to win a game are learned skills that can be just as rewarding.

**Seeing the Pitch** The greatest tool a hitter can have is good vision—the ability to recognize a pitch as it travels toward the plate. It begins in your stance by keeping both eyes level and focused on the pitcher. In softball, the ball will always be released from the hip, so don't let the pitcher's motion distract you from where the ball will be coming. Your hands should begin at the top of the strike zone, just in front of the rear shoulder. The strike zone is a rectangular area, the width of the plate, from your knees to your chest. It is the area in which you can hit the ball well if your timing is correct. If you don't swing and the ball travels through this zone, the umpire will call a strike. If the pitch is outside of this strike zone, a ball will be called.

**Hitting for Power** Hitting a long home run to win a game is any player's dream. Developing enough power in your swing to do so takes a combination of bat speed and strength and a commitment to perfecting it. A powerful swing begins by developing maximum rotation from the lower body. The energy generated from the legs is then transferred through the body to the arms and eventually through the bat at the point of contact.

As the pitcher releases the ball, your vision takes over and tells you to swing because this one looks like a strike. By waiting as long as possible, you see the ball for a greater period of time and can recognize the type of pitch and its location. As the ball approaches, your lower body begins to generate power by rotating, while your upper body stays still, with your hands remaining in a launching position. This movement causes a buildup of torque through your midsection, which is essential when hitting for power. As the energy is released through your arms, extend them to the point of contact. Also, make sure to snap your wrists just before contacting the ball, adding that last bit of bat speed.

Selecting the proper equipment also plays an important role in hitting home runs. As technology continues to improve, the responsiveness of the bat is allowing players that in the past wouldn't be able to hit the ball over the fence to do so regularly. Several years ago, manufacturers developed sophisticated metals that allow the bat to act like a trampoline and propel the ball with tremendous velocity.

**Hitting to the Opposite Field**  Pitchers often rely on throwing the ball to the outside part of the plate to get a batter out. Learning to hit this pitch to the opposite field (figure 7.2) is a sign of a great hitter, one that pitchers fear. When a pitcher throws a pitch to the outside portion of the plate, try to hit the ball in that direction, or to what is called the opposite field. Most players tend to pull the outside pitch, meaning they hit it to the same side of the field they are hitting from, resulting in a weak ground ball to an infielder. But by learning to recognize the ball's location and using the proper bat angle, you can achieve great success hitting to the opposite field.

Once again, seeing the ball and determining that it will be outside are vitally important. As you recognize the pitch, keep your hands back and allow the ball to get deeper into the hitting area, somewhere near home plate. On an inside pitch, the point of contact with the ball will be out in front of the plate, and the bat angle will cause you to pull the ball. By waiting on the outside pitch, you can then allow your hands to stay slightly in front of the ball, creating a bat angle that will direct it toward the opposite field.

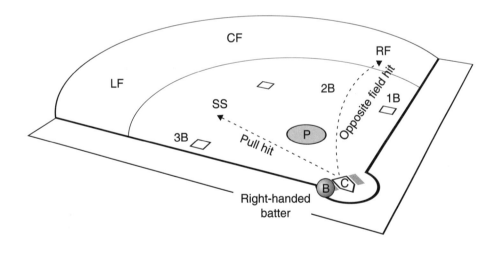

**7.2**  **Hit to opposite field compared to pull hit.**

**Hit and Run** Another offensive weapon coaches call on is the hit and run. With the player on first base running on the pitch, it is your job as the hitter to make contact with the ball. Ideally, you should hit a ground ball through the opening created by the infielder moving to cover the base of the advancing runner (figure 7.3). This means swinging down through the ball with a smooth stroke, making sure to hit a ground ball, rather than swinging as hard as you can. If the ball can get by the infielders, then the runner should have an excellent chance of advancing to third base. The hit and run is typically used only in special situations. The batter needs to be a good contact hitter that can be counted on, even on a bad pitch. In case the hitter doesn't make contact, the runner at first should possess good speed to give her a chance at stealing the base. In addition, the pitcher should face a count that forces her to throw a strike. When all of these factors exist, the hit and run can be a great tool.

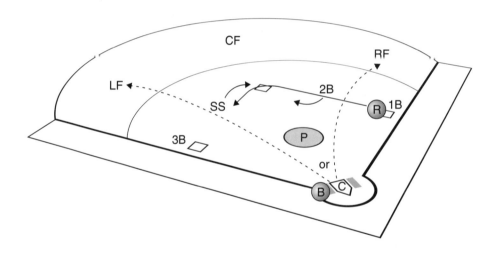

**7.3**    **Hit and run.**

**Fake Bunt and Hit**   Occasionally, you will face a team that brings their defensive players in very close to the hitter when a bunt situation is in order. (See chapter 8 for more about bunts.) By having these players so close, it gives you as the hitter an opportunity to more easily hit the ball by them. One technique is to square the bat around as if to bunt (figure 7.4a), but then pull it back as the pitcher releases the ball (figure 7.4b). With a smooth downward motion, hit a ground ball past the incoming defensive players (figure 7.4c), resulting in an easy base hit.

Fake Bunt and Hit

**7.4a**   **Square around as if to bunt.**

**7.4b**   **Pull back as pitcher releases the ball.**

**7.4c**   **Swing to hit the ball with full contact.**

## Establishing Strategy

Before stepping into the batter's box, you need to develop a strategy for each at-bat. The time in the game, the score, where and how many runners are on base, and most important, what your skills will allow you to do all factor into the plan. A good hitter realizes that his job changes depending on the situation and what the team needs him to accomplish up at the plate.

A strategy begins well before getting in the game to hit. It may involve talking about the pitcher with your coach or teammates before the game begins. You may have previous experience playing against her and can recall what type of pitches were thrown and where. Although you can never count on pitchers doing exactly the same thing, most will have a pattern they like to use and strengths that dictate their plan as well.

Your skills dictate what type of swing to use and the approach to take when hitting. If you have the speed to beat out a ground ball but not enough power to hit a home run, you would typically be called on to get on base and move runners around. Studying the pitcher's consistency is crucial; maybe by watching some pitches you can work the count for a walk. If you are a home run hitter that strikes out a lot, being more aggressive at the plate may be more appropriate.

If the pitcher likes to throw the ball on the outside part of the plate, then move in a little closer to reach the pitch more easily. As you see more pitches and their locations, adjust your position in the batter's box to improve your chances. If you are facing a pitcher that likes to throw drop balls, moving up to the front of the box can help you hit the ball before it drops out of the strike zone. If she throws rise balls, then move back in the box so as they move too high out of the strike zone, you can avoid swinging at them.

With runners on base, a coach could ask you to do a variety of things. If a runner is on first base, moving her to second and into scoring position could be crucial. In this case a bunt may be called for, or if you are a good contact hitter and the base runner has good speed, a hit and run could be called. A runner at second base can usually score on a base hit, but late in a game with nobody out, a coach may ask you to move the runner to third for an easier scoring opportunity. This could be accomplished with a bunt or a ground ball to the right side of the infield. A runner on third base can score in a variety of ways. If the pitcher is wild, you may want to take a few pitches to see if the runner can score on a wild pitch. Your strength may be hitting fly balls to the outfield, so with fewer than two outs a sacrifice fly would be an easy way of scoring the run.

You can employ numerous strategies as a hitter, but it all begins with a plan. Learn the tendencies of the pitcher, as well as the strengths of the opposing team. What do your strengths allow you to do, and what does the situation call for? By recognizing these factors, and having a strategy for each situation, your value to the team is immeasurable.

*Give it a go*

Hitting is one of the most difficult skills to master yet one of the easiest to practice. It could be as simple as watching yourself in a mirror swing a towel or a broom handle. Or, you could have automated machines and batting cages to use. Regardless of the equipment or facilities, practicing hitting takes concentration and hard work but in the end can pay off with improved results on the field.

## PROGRESSION DRILL

A basic drill that any team can employ, especially at the start of a season, is to begin with all of the team members in their stance and then progress step by step through a swing. First, take a step, checking balance and making sure there was limited weight shift and your hands stayed in a good launching position. Next, pivot your back foot, which allows for easier and more powerful rotation through the swing. Finally, use your hips and hands to finish the swing, maintaining balance but creating bat speed through the entire swing. This simple drill allows you to check for balance and proper fundamental technique through the entire swing without concentrating on hitting a ball. Once this drill is mastered you can add a ball on a tee, or ask another player to toss balls for the final swing phase to add complexity to the drill.

## BALANCE CHECK WITH HOP

Another simple drill for the beginning of the season enables you to check your balance before and after each swing. Before swinging the bat, get into your stance, then bend your knees and jump as high as you can in the air. As you come down, land on the balls of your feet in a good hitting position. If you are off balance when coming down, it is a good indicator that something should be changed to improve your stability. Next, swing the bat; hold the finish position to check for balance again and proper follow-through.

## TEE DRILLS

Using a tee to practice your basic hitting fundamentals or as a warm-up for a game can be extremely useful. First, set the ball in the middle of the strike zone about waist high. After mastering this position, change the tee to simulate an outside pitch, and hit the ball to the opposite field. Do the same for an inside pitch until these positions are mastered as well. You can also set the tee on a chair to practice high pitches, or shrink it down to simulate low pitches. Try these drills with your eyes closed to really feel how your swing is working and what needs to be changed.

## CENTER TOSS

A pitcher is not always available to throw batting practice; center toss, or front toss, is a perfect drill to simulate a live pitcher. A coach or player stands behind a screen about 20 to 25 feet (6.1 to 7.6 meters) away and tosses balls toward you, working on moving the ball to the inside part of the plate, then the outside. The coach can vary the speed of the pitch as well as the height. Because of the short distance, the timing is fairly similar to a live pitcher, and you can work on your weaknesses very effectively. Although it would always be best to hit off a live pitcher to simulate a game, using a coach for center toss is the next best thing.

# Bunting and Slap Hitting

**D**epending on your speed and hitting ability, you may want to tailor your offensive strategy around the short game. Bunting and slap hitting have become prevalent in the game of fastpitch softball because of the short distance between home plate and first base. If you have good foot speed but not a lot of power, then laying down a bunt and beating it out to first makes a lot of sense. By batting from the left-hand side of the batter's box, the distance to first has been reduced even further. When slap hitting, or drag bunting, you will be moving at contact with the ball, allowing even less time for the defense to make a play.

# Bunt

Whether the decision to bunt is made by you or the coach, it is important to not give the strategy away too early. Use the same stance you would use for hitting, although you should move toward the front of the batter's box. By moving up in the box, any ball that you bunt directly downward will be in fair territory. As the pitcher is about to release the ball, bring the bat around and extend your arms toward the pitcher. Slide your top hand up to the midpoint of the bat and pinch it with your thumb and index finger, making sure they stay out of the way of the ball. Create an angle with the bat by keeping the barrel end higher than the handle at all times (figure 8.1a).

Hold the bat high in the strike zone so that any adjustments to a lower pitch can be made in the downward direction. Keep the bat in the same position, relative to the body, and bend only your knees to make contact with a lower pitch. If contact is made with a low pitch by tilting the end of the bat to meet the ball, it can redirect the ball up toward your head.

**8.1a**    Set up for the bunt in the batter's box.

As the ball approaches, it is important to determine the location of the pitch. If the ball is on the inside part of the plate, right-handed players should direct the bunt down the third base line, left-handed players down the first base line. If you are right handed, direct an outside pitch down the first base line; if you are left handed, direct it down the third base line. Create an angle with the bat by moving the handle either back toward the catcher or forward toward the pitcher.

In most cases, when contact is made, you would like to cushion the impact by giving with the ball (figure 8.1b). This softens the blow and causes the ball to travel only a short distance, requiring the defensive players to go to the ball instead of the ball going to them. By doing this, you gain more time to beat the throw to first base or for other runners to advance safely.

**8.1b**  Cushion the impact by giving with the ball.

There are many different types of bunts, and selecting the most appropriate one is based on the situation and your skill level with each particular type. If the defensive players are anticipating the bunt and playing in close to the hitter, then a push bunt may be called for. When the defense is playing deep, a drag bunt is likely to result in a base hit. Practicing these various types of bunts will allow you to be a valuable and versatile player that a coach can use in virtually any situation.

**Sacrifice Bunt**  The most common type of bunt used to advance runners into scoring position is the sacrifice bunt (figure 8.2). With this strategy, you sacrifice your out at first base to allow the runner to advance to the next base. As the pitcher is about to release the ball, square around and face her by adjusting your feet. You can do this by completely changing your position in the box or by pivoting on the balls of your feet. Make sure the bat is out in front of the plate and in position to "catch" the ball. Only bunt the ball if it is a strike, and remember to bend your knees to meet a low pitch rather than reach with your arms. Angle the bat so the ball goes down one of the baselines, depending on whether the pitch is inside or outside. It is important that you properly execute the bunt before trying to beat the throw to first base.

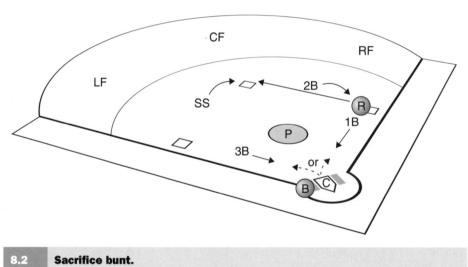

**8.2**   **Sacrifice bunt.**

**Drag Bunt**  If the defense is not expecting the bunt and playing a little deeper than they should, a drag bunt (figure 8.3) is an excellent offensive strategy. With this bunt, you are bunting for a base hit, so timing and getting out of the box are crucial. Wait as long as possible before squaring around to bunt so that you don't give away your intention. Slide your top hand up the barrel of the bat while bringing the bat in front of the plate. For right-handed hitters, drop your right foot back away from the plate so you are in more of a sprinter's stance. As the ball arrives, bunt down through the ball in a rowing motion, making sure to direct it down a baseline. As contact is made, quickly accelerate down the first base line.

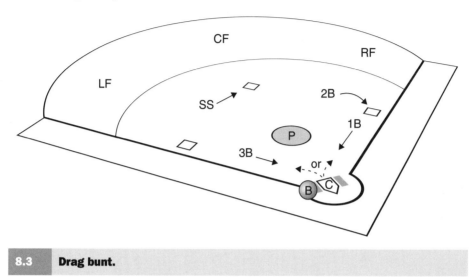

**8.3** Drag bunt.

**Push Bunt** If the defense is playing in close, a push bunt (figure 8.4) could be used. Square around early as if to sacrifice bunt, but instead of softly catching the ball with the bat, push through it. Extend the bat quickly, making solid contact with the ball, almost as if hitting it but with the control of a bunt. The ball needs to go between the pitcher and either the third or first baseman. If you get the ball past these oncoming defensive players, you should be able to beat out the bunt for a base hit.

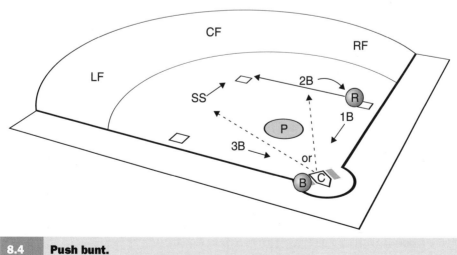

**8.4** Push bunt.

**Squeeze Bunt**   With a runner on third base with good speed, you may choose to employ a squeeze bunt (figure 8.5). As the pitcher releases the ball, the runner from third breaks for home, relying on you to make contact with the ball. Square around as the ball is released, realizing that you must bunt the ball even if it is not a strike. It is also crucial to make the ball go down; popping it up in the air will allow the defense to easily throw out the runner trying to get back to third base.

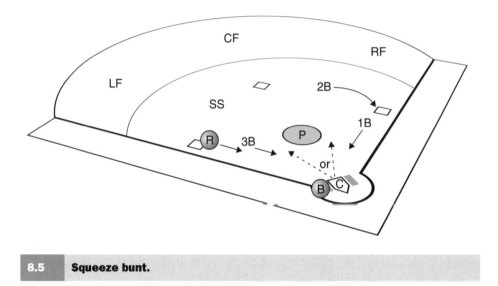

**8.5**   **Squeeze bunt.**

**Slap Hitting**   Another short-game strategy is slap hitting. You always slap as a left-handed hitter, running toward the ball as it comes from the pitcher. If you are not naturally left handed, then standing in this side of the batter's box can feel awkward at first, but with time it will become second nature. Begin toward the back of the box to give you plenty of room to run forward as the ball approaches. As with your normal hitting stance, start with your feet slightly wider than your shoulders, the hands in front of your rear shoulder, and both eyes focused on the pitcher's hip, watching for the release of the ball.

As the ball is released, take a small timing step backward with your right foot (figure 8.6a). Next, take a large crossover step with your left foot, making sure to stay in line with the pitcher (figure 8.6b). Keep your left foot closed by pointing it toward third base during this crossover. As this foot is landing, bring the bat to the contact point by keeping your hands inside of the ball and the bat at an angle to direct the ball toward the shortstop area (figure 8.6c). Your goal with most pitches is to hit a ground ball past the third baseman, requiring the shortstop to make a difficult backhand play. You can also use this technique for a drag bunt. Instead of slapping at the ball, bring the bat out in front of the plate and softly catch the ball with the bat. This is a very effective tool if you are a fast runner and have good eye–hand coordination.

## Slap Hit

8.6a **Take a small step backward.**

8.6b **Crossover step with the other foot.**

8.6c **Bring bat forward to make contact.**

# Scoping the Opponent

You can adopt numerous strategies with the short game, and finding the one that is appropriate for each situation can be difficult. Before deciding on a plan of action, evaluate the personnel involved. First, what are your skills? Do you have the ability to put down a perfect squeeze bunt when called for or the speed to beat out a drag bunt? How fast are the base runners? Also, consider game situations, such as the score and the inning. If the score is close and it's late in the game, moving a runner into scoring position becomes extremely important.

The most difficult factor to consider is the defensive team's players. Unless you have scouted them thoroughly, it will be difficult to know their strengths and weaknesses. The pregame warm-up is an excellent time to watch how they move and how quickly they get rid of the ball during their throws. If your team can find a player with a potential weakness, testing her early in the game could be a key.

It is generally easiest to consider the defensive team's positioning when creating a strategy. A third baseman who plays a little deep presents a great opportunity for dropping down a drag bunt. If he plays in extremely close with runners on base, then a push bunt is in order. If he plays in close and likes to throw to second base to get the runner out on a bunt, you may want to bunt and run.

It takes a combination of understanding your abilities and the defensive players' talent and positions to formulate a strategy. Using the short game puts pressure on the defensive team to make the play. If they don't handle the play well, it can give your team momentum to score some runs. It is also valuable when facing an extremely good pitcher that your team is having difficulty hitting.

Developing bunting skills used in the short game is much easier than becoming a home run hitter, so practicing these tactics can lead to a lot of success. Executing a bunt in a crucial situation takes a lot of concentration and confidence. Developing the confidence begins during practice while mastering the skill of bunting.

## BUNTING OFF A MACHINE

One of the best ways to learn how to bunt is using a pitching machine. It throws a strike every time and gives you many repetitions in a short time period. You can even set some machines to simulate drop balls or rise balls, making it more gamelike. After you have learned the basic skill of bunting, use the machine to create competition among your teammates. Have a partner call out a type of bunt just before putting the ball into the machine. If you execute it properly, you get rewarded with points; if you don't, points are taken away from your score. The person with the most points at the end of practice is the winner.

## COLORED BALL DRILL

Ask another player to toss two different colored balls at you, or use two pitching machines. As the balls get close, the other player yells out a color for you to bunt. Quickly determine the correct color and bunt only that ball. It takes a great deal of concentration to watch two balls coming at you and then pick the appropriate one.

## BROOM HANDLE BUNT

Use a cut-down broom handle or a similarly designed bat to practice your bunting. The smaller diameter makes it more difficult to execute the bunt and improves your concentration. Because of the increased difficulty, use a Wiffle ball or safety ball for this drill. A coach can toss the balls, or you can use live pitching or a machine to simulate game situations. Make this drill more difficult by calling out the intended location of the bunt before contacting the ball.

## TARGET GAME

A good drill that creates competition within the team is a bunting contest to hit specific spots with your bunts. Lay out some targets on the ground with jump ropes (figure 8.7). Each team member gets the same number of opportunities, and points are awarded for each ball that is bunted into the target area. As you get more skilled, make these target areas smaller and more difficult to keep the ball inside of. You could also use a variety of sized targets, with smaller ones being worth more points than larger ones.

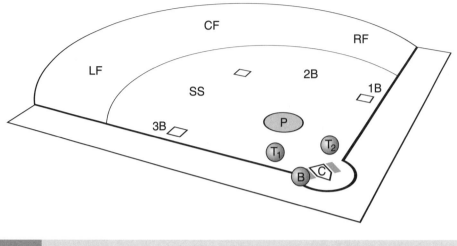

**8.7**     **Target game.**

## GLOVE CATCH

To teach someone to slap hit for the first time, especially a normally right-handed hitter, this drill is excellent. Put on a fielder's glove, and get into your regular hitting stance. Ask someone to pitch a ball to you. Go through the slap hitting footwork, catching the ball at the appropriate contact point. Practice this with a live pitcher or a pitching machine at increased speeds to get the feel for the appropriate footwork. By catching the ball at the contact point, you will learn the fundamental skill of slap hitting without the frustration of not hitting the ball.

# Baserunning

One of the most neglected skills in the game of softball is baserunning. A lot of time in most practices is spent on hitting, pitching, and defensive skills, with little time dedicated to the skill of baserunning. Most people would assume you need great speed to be a good base runner. But, just like any other aspect of the game, baserunning is a learned skill and needs to be practiced. If you have a lot of speed but little knowledge of baserunning, your usefulness is limited. Successful teams will win games with good baserunning, and often it isn't the fastest runner that makes a difference but the one that takes advantage of a situation when it arises.

Developing greater running speed through weightlifting and other training regimens is an important part of improving, but watching the tendencies and abilities of the opposing team can also make a difference. A smart runner will learn which opposing players have weaker throwing arms, opening up the opportunity to take another base. Sometimes coaches and teams will show specific tendencies as to which bases they like to throw to and when. A good base runner will learn from these and look for opportunities to take advantage of these plays.

# Run the Bases!

Whether you are leaving the batter's box or first base, an explosive first step is crucial. Your stride must initially be short and then lengthen as momentum is generated. Because of this, the quicker player holds an advantage over the faster player when running from base to base. Push off the ground with your toes, increasing stride length with each step (figure 9.1a). Maintaining a low center of gravity during these initial stages of running is a must and allows you to stay balanced. It can also be helpful to feel as if you were falling forward toward your destination, causing your feet to move more quickly to catch up and prevent falling.

As you begin to lengthen your stride, stand up a little taller while maintaining the forward lean. Land on your toes, making contact

**9.1a**   **Push off with toes.**

with the ground for as little time as possible (figure 9.1b). Increase your speed by moving your arms in a rhythmic fashion and driving them forward and back with each stride. Your hands should be relaxed and should approach the side of your face on the upswing and pass behind your hips on the downswing. If you tend to tighten up your fists and arms while running, it can actually slow you down by creating tension throughout your body.

Run in a straight line whenever possible, keeping the distance you are traveling to a minimum. As you pass a base, keep your stride and hit the front corner of the base with your foot (figure 9.1c). As you round a base, try to keep the distance around the base as short as possible.

**9.1b**    **Lengthen stride and run tall.**

**9.1c**    **Hit base with front foot.**

During the course of a game, numerous baserunning situations occur. By preparing for these with practice, you can make the difference between safe or out and winning or losing a game. These skills take practice just as any other, and although not glamorous, they are usually the difference in a game.

**Leading Off**   After you have safely made it to a base, your next obvious goal is to get to the next one as soon as possible. Being able to lead off the base as the ball is pitched is a tremendous advantage when used properly. There are generally two types of leadoffs, the rocker start and the push-off method. In the push-off style, one foot is on the base, ready to use it as leverage to push against, and the other is extended toward the next base (figure 9.2). This option gives you a stride length of distance off the base. When the ball is released by the pitcher, take your lead by allowing the foot to come off the base.

**9.2**   **Push-off method of leading off.**

The more common method used to lead off is the rocker lead. Your left foot is on the inside part of the base, once again using it for leverage, as a sprinter would use starting blocks in track. The right foot is behind the base, and your body is in an athletic position awaiting the delivery of the pitch. As the pitcher begins her motion, put most of your weight on the back foot by leaning in that direction. Before the ball is released, drive your body forward by pushing off with the back foot. As you begin your sprinting motion, time the release of the pitch with your front foot leaving the base (figure 9.3). If your foot leaves the base before the pitcher releases the ball, then you can be called out. The advantage with this lead is that you are moving with the pitch, creating momentum and gaining an edge when trying to steal a base or when reacting to a ground ball.

When leading off of first base, regardless of the style, generally take three strides off of the base. Any more than that and you become an easy target for the catcher to pick off with a throw. As you take your third stride, square your body to the catcher, making sure you can move either way quickly. From second base, a longer lead is possible because of the greater distance from the catcher. Take a five-step lead until you square up to the catcher, and you should be safe from any potential throws in that direction. At third base, a three-step lead is usually enough, and because of the potential of tagging up on a fly ball, you usually aren't as aggressive leading off of third base.

**9.3**    **Rocker method of leading off.**

**Tagging Up**   When a fly ball is caught with fewer than two outs, you have the opportunity to tag up and advance one base or more. You cannot leave the base until the ball has been caught, and if you do leave early, you can be called out. The defensive team can also get you out by applying a tag before reaching the base. Determining which fly balls will allow you to safely advance depends on running speed and the base you are on. You would not typically tag up at first base, unless you are extremely fast and the ball was hit deep into the outfield. At second base, the option of advancing to third is more likely, and a fly ball hit to deep center or medium depth to right field would allow most runners to advance easily. It is more common to tag up at third base, with the ability to score a run on most fly balls to the outfield.

After the ball is hit in the air to the outfielder, return to the base as quickly as possible. Establish a good athletic position with one foot on the base before the ball is caught. If possible, try to get into the regular leadoff position, and anticipate the ball being caught. Just before it is caught, get your momentum moving toward the next base, and time it so that your foot leaves the base with the catch. As a player, you should always expect to advance to the next base; allow the base coach to make any decision to stop you.

**Rounding the Base**   A good base runner does not rely solely on speed to be successful but practices proper baserunning techniques. Finding the shortest distance between two points is a crucial geometry lesson for a base runner. Often a runner will take a wide sweeping arc when rounding a base, wasting valuable time covering a greater distance. It is important to set up a good angle when approaching the base by simulating the shape of a parenthesis—gradually move to the right of the base and then back to the inside corner of the base as you hit it (figure 9.4). As you approach the base, lower your center of gravity by dipping the inside shoulder down, allowing you to make a sharper turn. After passing the base, forge a straight path to the next one, keeping in mind the geometry lesson of the shortest distance between two points.

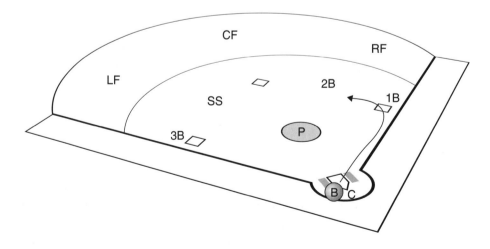

**9.4**   **Path around the bases.**

# Stealing a Base

Another way to advance is to steal a base. Of course you are not removing it from the field but advancing the base without the hitter doing anything to move you over. To be successful at stealing a base, you need to possess a certain amount of foot speed. In addition, the timing of leaving the base, the type of pitch and its location, the ability of the other team to get to the base, and the catcher's release and arm strength all factor into your success. Being just one step late with the release of the pitch is often the difference between being safe or out.

Using the rocker lead discussed earlier allows you to have your momentum going at the release of the pitch, giving you an advantage over waiting to move until the ball is let go. As you leave the base, run in a straight line toward the outside corner of the base you are trying to steal. Keep your eyes on the defensive player, who is getting ready to catch the throw. Usually, he will set up inside of the base, making the outside corner the most desirable spot to reach for. If the throw is off line, the defensive player will move to the ball, which requires you to adjust your sliding point.

Many base stealers like to slide headfirst, which can be a quicker way of getting to the base but requires that you avoid contact with the defensive player. A serious injury can occur if you slide directly into the defensive player with your head. Slide an arm's length away from the base, staying away from any direct contact and making it difficult to be tagged out. When sliding feetfirst, it is important to recognize whether the play is going to be close or not. If the defensive player is delayed in catching the ball, slide directly into the base. If you see the catch being made before you get to the base, slide to the side, away from the tag, and either hook the base with your foot as you go past or grab it with your hand. By sliding away from the defensive player, you make it hard for her to apply a tag, and you could sneak in safely.

Scouting the defensive team's players is important for being a successful base stealer. If the catcher has a quick release of the ball and a strong, accurate throwing arm, it will be difficult to steal a base. You may need to watch the pitcher and be able to recognize when she is going to throw a change-up, and then try to steal. Defensive players covering the base to receive the throw can also determine when you try to steal. Some players concentrate too long on the batter and are late getting to the base to cover it. Becoming a good base stealer takes a lot of concentration and anticipation in addition to having natural foot speed. By recognizing the tendencies of the opposing team, you won't have to rely just on speed to be successful.

Developing your speed can help you improve as a player. Various strength and conditioning programs are vital for speed development, but practice drills that focus on running form and technique can be just as beneficial. Although natural talent will determine a player's speed and quickness more than anything else, anyone can gain some speed and quickness through strength training and practice. Most of these drills can be accomplished on your own, but it helps to have a workout partner who can critique your technique and push you through to the end.

## POWER SKIPS

Power skips will help you develop the explosiveness needed to steal a base or score from second on a base hit. Start by standing still and lifting your left knee straight up in the air, keeping it bent. At the same time, drive your right arm up while keeping it at 90 degrees. Now, while standing still, practice going back and forth between sides, lifting the right leg and left arm, then the left leg and right arm. Once you have the rhythm of the movement, start driving your limbs up higher and higher so that you lift yourself off the ground. The final sequence is to do this action in a skipping motion, making sure to concentrate on lifting yourself off the ground rather than moving forward, although you will certainly gain ground with each jump.

## FOUL POLES

If you have access to a field, especially one with a warning track and foul poles, this drill will help you develop stride length and power. A softball field has two foul poles that mark the out-of-play line at the outfield fence, one in right field and the other in left. A warning track is the area between the two poles just in front of the outfield fence; it is usually made of dirt so that a player feels the difference under her feet when approaching the fence.

Find a partner with roughly the same leg length as yours. Start at one foul pole, following the curvature of the outfield fence. Begin running slowly while emphasizing staying side by side with your partner and matching stride length. Drive your lead leg up and out, reaching farther as you gain speed. At about the halfway point, you should be overexaggerating your stride length so that both feet are off the ground at the same time in kind of a prancing motion.

Continue to try to match your partner's stride, running past the opposite foul pole. During this drill, concentrate on staying on your toes and pumping your arms. Try to keep your head still by focusing on a distant object.

## LADDERS

To develop foot speed and agility, you can use a running ladder to practice a variety of drills. A running ladder is two pieces of parallel rope with flat rungs spread equally between the ends. Lay the ladder out flat and straight on even, level ground or flooring. You can get creative when doing these drills and come up with your own ideas, but here are several to practice with. First do a two-foot hop, landing with both feet between the rungs. Go as quickly as you can, trying to land only on your toes. Next, run with high knees; again put both feet down between the rungs. Turn sideways to the ladder and do the same drill, working on staying low and moving your feet quickly. Now do the two-foot hopping drill, first into a rung and then back out and forward into the second rung and back out. Keep this pattern all the way down the ladder, concentrating on quick feet and balance.

## FOUR BASE DRILL

Practicing the running techniques you will use in a game is very important as well. When practicing with a team, everyone can be divided into four groups, with each practicing a different technique from one base to the next. If a player simulates a pitch from the circle, just as in a game, the first person at each base can work on her timing. The line of players standing at home plate practices running through first base. Work on increasing stride length down the line, hitting the front side of the base, running through it without slowing, and finally breaking down into an athletic position after passing the base. The group running from first to second practices stealing a base. A couple of options exist for the runners going from second to third. You could practice a hit and run, or if there is extra help around, a coach can hit ground balls to a shortstop so you can practice which ground balls allow you to get to third base. The runners going from third to home practice tagging up on fly balls and getting a proper jump on the catch. It's best if coaches are available to simulate an actual fly ball, but if not, just visualize the play.

# Sliding

**O**ften considered one of the most dangerous skills in the game of fastpitch softball, sliding causes many young players apprehension. However with practice, proper equipment, and good facilities, sliding becomes just another part of the game that can mean the difference between winning and losing. Safety bases that allow you to slide over the base or that break free when contacted can prevent injury. A sprained ankle can result when you slide late into a stationary base that doesn't give with the contact. It is also important that the ground around the base be taken care of before the game. If the field is used often and not raked out between games, a divot can form in front of a base, causing a potential hazard.

Wearing protective gear can also prevent injury. Kneepads and sliding shorts can prevent abrasions from contacting the dirt; using braces or taping your ankles can also be a tremendous help. Problems often occur when you hesitate or are indecisive about sliding, so always run hard and slide with confidence. By preparing yourself with the right equipment and practicing the various techniques discussed in this chapter, you will learn to slide with confidence.

# Feetfirst Slide

Although there are many different ways to slide, the most important thing to remember is that in order to slide, you need to be moving fast. Many players tend to slow down as they prepare to slide, causing them to end up short of the base or to stumble, resulting in an awkward landing into the base. A good base runner uses many sliding variations to either deceive the defensive player or gain an advantage.

The most common sliding method, sometimes called the bent-leg technique and often considered the safest way to slide, is feetfirst straight into the base. Begin by running in a straight line toward the base (figure 10.1a). As you approach it, lower your center of gravity by bending at the knees (figure 10.1b); just before reaching the base, extend one leg and bring the opposite foot toward the inside of the knee. Your legs should be shaped like the number four (figure 10.1c). Contact the ground by landing on your backside; lean back,

**10.1a**  Run straight toward the base.

**10.1b**  Lower center of gravity by bending the knees.

extending your arms and keeping your chin tucked to your chest. As contact is made with the base, allow your knee to bend, absorbing the force of the collision. Some players like to contact the ground with their knees rather than their backsides, which can help with the pop-up slide discussed later in the chapter.

The timing of when to slide depends on several different factors including your running speed, the conditions of the field, and your approach into the base. The more speed you have as you approach the base, the sooner you can slide. A field that is soft and made of sand will slow you down sooner and therefore requires a later slide. By recognizing the condition of the field, you can adjust your timing. The final variable to consider is where your foot will contact the base. If you are sliding directly into the base, then you can slide a little earlier than if you are planning on sliding to the outside and past the base to avoid the tag.

**10.1c**　**Extend one leg to base.**

When the situation calls for different sliding techniques, it is important to have practiced them. An injury can result if you attempt a slide that is inappropriate for the situation or if you are not skilled enough to perform it. A headfirst slide can be a valuable tool, but it can also be dangerous if you slide directly into the defensive player. Most variations of the basic sliding skill are designed to avoid the tag by taking an indirect line into the base, including the hook slide and various slide-by techniques.

**Pop-Up Slide**   A slight variation on the bent-leg slide is to quickly get off the ground, anticipating the possibility of advancing another base. This pop-up slide is useful when the throw is mishandled by a player or an overthrow occurs while you are sliding into the base. As you hit the base, push off of the ground with the bent leg, using momentum to pop up into a running position (figure 10.2). To help lift your body up, you can also push off the ground with a hand. When using the pop-up slide, having enough running speed is the most crucial factor. Make sure that as little of your body hits the ground as possible, reducing the amount of friction and allowing you to pop up out of the slide.

**10.2    Pop-up slide.**

**Hook Slide**   When you anticipate a close play at a base, one technique you can use is the hook slide. It is similar to the bent-leg slide, but instead of sliding directly into the base, you slide past it while maintaining contact with your foot. Usually, you will slide to the outside of the base, but a throw coming from the outfield could mean a slide to the inside. The defensive player receiving the throw from the outfield will typically stand to the outside of the base, which allows you to avoid the tag by sliding to the inside. Pick your intended landing point, extend your lead leg, and allow the foot of the other leg to bend to the outside, hooking it on the corner of the base (figure 10.3). Stay low to avoid the tag, and if your foot comes off of the base, grab the base with your hand as you slide by.

**10.3**   **Hook slide.**

**Headfirst Slide**   Although considered a very dangerous technique, when done correctly in the proper situation, using the headfirst slide can be a great tool for the base runner. When sliding headfirst, never slide directly into the base or the defensive player. Injuries can result when contact is made with the head or shoulders into the player trying to make the tag. Sliding headfirst into home should be avoided in nearly every circumstance. A catcher with protective gear should be avoided at all costs, so using a feetfirst method is much safer when sliding into home plate.

As you approach the base, note the location of the defensive player and try to slide away from where he has set up to receive the ball. Because you have a full arm's length to reach the base, you may choose to take a line a couple of feet outside the base. Lower your center of gravity by bending at the knees and the waist, extending your arms and body toward the chosen path. Keep your hands clenched to help prevent any injuries to your fingers. Land on your abdomen and waist, making sure to keep your chin up and preferably turning your head away from the incoming throw (figure 10.4). Grab the corner of the base as you slide by, staying low to avoid the tag.

**10.4** **Headfirst slide.**

**Slide-By**   With the slide-by technique, use a feetfirst slide but pick a point away from the tag and grab it with your hand as you slide by the base. Choose a path to the base away from the defensive player, using the standard bent-leg skill. Slide a little closer to the base than you normally would, while anticipating that your momentum will carry you past the base. Stay low to avoid the tag, and grab the base with your hand as you slide past. Occasionally, you will roll onto your side during this skill, which could expose your face to injury from the ball or an aggressive tag.

# Anticipating Close Plays

A base runner can steal a base or score the winning run when she makes a good slide. Conversely, a poor slide can result in an out or a missed scoring opportunity. When a play is close at a base, you must be able to avoid the tag, a learned skill you should practice whenever possible. First you need to anticipate a close play. As you approach the base, read the body language of the defensive player; you can usually tell by her actions if a close play is coming.

Next, note the location of the defensive player so you can adjust your approach into the base. If he is set up on the inside of the base and the ball is coming from the same side, angle for the outside of the base. If a defensive player sets up on the inside of the base when the throw is coming from the outfield, it usually means the throw is high. Again, slide away from the player to the outside of the base, but anticipate a poor throw and be ready to advance another base. The same idea applies if the player is on the outside of the base when the throw is coming from the inside. Slide away from the player, but anticipate an overthrow.

If the player catches the ball well before you begin your slide, there are a couple of options you can employ. It is important that you avoid a collision at any cost since the injuries that could result are not worth the extra base or run. Most of the time, the defensive player will be on the side of the base nearest the throw and will be anticipating your sliding away from her. On close plays, taking a wide angle around the defender and reaching in with a hand or foot at the last second is possible. But, when the player has the ball and is anticipating your path to the base, fake a move away from her and at the last moment change your direction. Some players will be caught by surprise, anticipating your slide to the outside. The player will usually shift her weight, anticipating making the tag away from the base, which allows you to slip by safely to the inside.

Another option, although rarely attempted, is to jump over the player. Once again, it is more effective when the player has just caught the ball and is trying to locate you to make a tag. You can surprise him by jumping straight up and over his tag, but keep in mind that he could stand up, causing you to flip over and resulting in a dangerous play.

It is difficult to practice sliding without feeling a little scared or apprehensive. Usually the field is hard and can cause bruises, bumps, and scrapes with repetitive sliding. Finding a way to practice sliding in a safe environment is important to perfect the various sliding techniques and gain confidence in your skills.

## RUNNING WITH COACHES

If you are just learning how to slide, have two coaches hold each of your hands and run with you toward the base. As you prepare to slide, the coaches will continue to carry your weight, allowing you to be gradually lowered to the ground. As you become more comfortable with the idea, the coaches can allow more weight to hit the ground, until you are landing on your own.

## SLIDE RITE

The fear of injury makes practicing sliding difficult, but using a protective pad can help alleviate the fear. A Slide Rite features a foam pad covered in nylon, with an extra piece of material on top that moves freely on the covering. As you slide on the top sheet, the padding cushions the impact and the material gives, allowing for a safe slide. Practice all the different sliding techniques, making sure to wear a helmet and other protective gear if needed. You can move this pad into game situations as well. It is a great tool when working on stealing bases or practicing throw-downs from the catcher, when repetitive slides are required.

## SLIP AND SLIDE

A fun way to practice sliding is to use a piece of plastic with water on it. Set the piece of plastic, with plenty of standing water on it, just in front of the base, near where you would start a slide. Begin your slide at the edge of the plastic—if you try to run on the wet plastic, you could accidentally slip and injure yourself. If you don't want to get wet, and a Slide Rite is not available, set up a piece of cardboard in the grass. Run to the edge of the cardboard and then go into your slide. The cardboard should slide easily on the grass without damaging it.

## ALL SLIDE DRILL

To get used to sliding, as well as receive some conditioning, start at home plate and run around the bases as you normally would, except slide at every base. At first base practice the standard feetfirst slide directly into the base. Get up and head for second, where you slide headfirst to the outside of the base as if stealing and avoiding the tag. Quickly get up and race to third, where you practice a pop-up slide. Finally, run to home plate and slide by the base to the side, pretending to avoid an imaginary tag. This drill is great practice and a difficult workout that can make any player tired.

# Offensive Tactics

**O**ne of the most appealing aspects of fastpitch softball is the variety of opportunities it provides. Players of all shapes and sizes can contribute to offensive success when they are used in the proper way. A team made up of small but quick players may use a lot of bunting, slap hitting, and base stealing to score runs. A team that is large and powerful at the plate may depend on home runs.

It is up to the coach to find a strategy that best uses the players on the team. Asking a small but fast player to hit the ball over the fence is not realistic and would most likely cause the player to become frustrated with the game. A player who understands and anticipates the appropriate strategy for any given situation has a tremendous advantage. This is called *game sense*, and it comes after years of playing and observing the game at all levels. Coaches love players with game sense on their teams because these players can act as coaches on the field.

# Creating the Lineup

Developing an offensive strategy for a game begins with the coach putting players in a batting order that maximizes each player's ability and presents the greatest opportunity for scoring runs. The coach must look at the entire roster and recognize the strengths and weaknesses of the team. For example, a coach who is lucky enough to have nine strong offensive players in the lineup might want to alternate players who are slower and faster on the base paths to make it more difficult for the defensive team to defend them. However rarely is a team stacked with hitters, so the challenge for the coach is to find the proper spot in the batting order for each player. Usually a team is composed of players with varying skill and athletic ability.

The leadoff hitter is the player who can be trusted to get on base more than any other player on the team. This player usually has good running speed and can steal bases or move into scoring position with a sacrifice bunt. More important, the leadoff hitter should have a lot of confidence, be able to see a lot of pitches, and be willing to get on base via a walk. A player who likes to swing at anything and strikes out a lot is probably not the best option for the leadoff hitter.

A player who has good speed and can hit consistently is a good choice for the second slot in the lineup. This player needs to be able to perform sacrifice bunts to move the leadoff hitter into scoring position. She can't get too anxious at the plate and must have the ability to watch some pitches before swinging at just the right one. The second hitter needs to be patient at the plate to allow the leadoff hitter a chance to steal a base, even if it means getting behind in the count.

The third hitter in the lineup must possess the ability to drive in runs and put the ball in play when asked. This hitter is usually the most consistent and talented hitter in the lineup. The third hitter needs to be aggressive at the plate and find a way to drive in runners on base.

The fourth hitter, sometimes called the cleanup hitter, also is one of the best hitters on the team but probably will strike out more often. The fourth hitter should be able to generate a great deal of power to hit for extra bases and drive in runs.

The hitter in the fifth slot also must be a very good hitter but usually does not have as much power as the fourth hitter. The fifth hitter should possess a little more speed to give the team a scoring opportunity if the top of the lineup doesn't score any runs.

The sixth hitter is very similar to the fifth hitter but usually does not have the power to produce a lot of extra-base hits. The seventh and eighth hitters typically have the lowest batting averages in the lineup. Depending on the type of players on the team, these hitters may be very powerful but strike out often or may have little power or speed.

Many people mistakenly believe that the last hitter in the lineup should be the weakest. The ninth hitter shouldn't be the weakest hitter because the best hitters on the team are coming up next. This batter must be able to get on base and score runs for the team. He should be another leadoff-type hitter who can get on base, has the speed to steal a base, and can work well with the top of the order. The ninth hitter usually does not have the high batting average or the discipline of a leadoff hitter, but he is crucial to the success of the team.

Remember, these are just guidelines for putting together a lineup; every team is different. (See table 11.1 for a summary of batting order strengths and weaknesses.) The most successful coaches find

**Table 11.1**

## BATTING ORDER STRENGTHS AND WEAKNESSES

| Order in lineup | Speed | Power | Average and hitting strategy |
|---|---|---|---|
| Leadoff hitter | Usually fastest player on the team | Limited power | Should have a good on-base percentage and the patience to take a lot of pitches and find a way to get on base |
| Second hitter | One of the fastest players on the team | Limited power but should have the ability to lay down a sacrifice bunt | Good, patient hitter who may take some pitches to give the leadoff hitter a chance to steal a base |
| Third hitter | Speed varies; usually a good athlete with above-average speed | Excellent power but doesn't sacrifice power for strikeouts | Best hitter on the team; drives in runners and hits for a high average |
| Fourth hitter | Usually average to below-average speed | Excellent power; may strikeout more than most hitters | Lower average; is in the lineup to hit the ball hard and drive in runs |
| Fifth hitter | Doesn't require great speed | Good power; can drive in runs when needed | Good, balanced hitter; drives in runs and hits for average |
| Sixth hitter | Usually average speed | Can have good power depending on hitting philosophy | Usually a streaky hitter who has a lower average but can come through with a big hit |
| Seventh hitter | Average to above-average speed | Typically a little less power than hitters in the middle of the lineup | Lower average |
| Eighth hitter | Average to above-average speed | Not much power | Low batting average; usually a good defensive player who has to have a spot in the lineup |
| Ninth hitter | Good to excellent speed | Limited power | Second leadoff hitter who can find a way to get on base |

a way to get players to work together in a lineup that makes sense and lets players work off each other's strengths. Some hitters are more comfortable in one spot in the lineup than another. The coach must talk and work with players to find out what they think are their best spots and why. The coach may need to do some convincing if a player's opinion differs from the coach's, but the coach should be able to explain the reason for her decision. Finding consistency in the batting order can be difficult, but it is a crucial part of the coach's job.

For the coach to use various strategies to create runs, players must get on base. Once players get on base, the ways in which a team can score runs are virtually endless. Many coaches have great ideas about scoring runs, but the first order of business is to find a way to get some base runners.

# Executing the Hit and Run

The hit and run (see figure 7.3, page 76) requires the right players and a lot of trust. When a runner is on either first or second, the hitter should anticipate being asked to hit the next pitch, regardless of location. Essentially the runner will try to steal the base, causing the infielders to follow the runner in anticipation of a throw from the catcher. The hitter's job is to find the hole created by the steal, hitting a ground ball to that spot. Because the defensive players are out of alignment, the ball has a good chance of rolling through the infield for a base hit, allowing the runner to advance an additional base quite easily.

If anything goes wrong with the strategy, all the players involved must react accordingly. The runner must always check to see where the ball is going as she steals the base. If the hitter pops the ball in the air, the runner needs to get back to the starting base before the defense can throw or tag her out. The hitter must be able to handle the pitch properly. The hitter needs to understand that fouling off a difficult pitch is a better option than popping out to an infielder. When executed properly, the hit and run is a tremendous offensive tool that can help the runner and the hitter be more successful.

# Taking Extra Bases

Players who possess good running speed may be able to take advantage of defensive miscues to get more bases than they are entitled to. A smart base runner who can read the defense is likely to take many more extra bases. Opportunities to advance a base or get on base present themselves in every game.

For example, if a hitter strikes out but the catcher misses the ball, the hitter can try to reach first base safely. Usually the hitter is so preoccupied with striking out that he forgets to run until it is too late and the catcher has made the play.

A runner who reaches first base safely should glance toward second base to see if a defensive player is covering second. Sometimes the defensive players get so caught up in the moment, they forget to pay attention to the safe base runner, especially after a close play. If no one is covering second and the play hasn't ended yet, a smart base runner will take advantage of the opportunity and quickly advance to the next base.

First base provides several opportunities to advance an extra base. The runner at first should read the ball off the bat as the next hitter hits it. The runner should realize that a base hit to right field presents an excellent opportunity for him to get to third base. A bunt may leave third base uncovered, allowing the runner to advance all the way from first to third.

A runner at second base may be able to tag up and advance on a foul ball or even score by tagging up on a deep fly ball. A runner from second often will score on a base hit. When this happens, the hitter should end up at second if the defense allows the throw to go all the way to home plate in an attempt to prevent the run. Base runners should always anticipate the play and react to an opportunity.

# Stealing Bases

One of the greatest tools available to an offense is the ability to steal bases. Of course, any successful base stealing team will have players with good speed, but strategy is part of success as well. The coach must know the speed of the team's base stealers and the time it takes for each stealer to get from first to second from the release of the pitch. Knowing how long it takes the catcher to get the ball to second base also determines how successful base stealers will be. The coach should do some scouting before creating the game plan.

The other part of the equation when stealing bases is anticipating a certain type of pitch or the pitch location. Knowing when a pitcher will throw a change-up can make stealing a base much easier. The drop ball is another good pitch for a base runner to steal on. Even a good drop ball often ends up in the dirt, making it difficult for the catcher to throw out a quick base stealer.

Certain game situations call for an attempt at a stolen base. With two outs and a runner on first, getting the runner into scoring position is critical, and stealing a base is a good way to do it. A leadoff hitter who gets on base is a good candidate to attempt a steal, especially if the defensive team is looking for a sacrifice bunt or a hit and run. A double steal (figure 11.1) is also a valuable weapon. It is difficult for the defensive team to defend a double steal if they are worrying about a bunt or slap hit. The shortstop doesn't want to leave her position early, and the third baseman is playing up, relying on the shortstop to get to the base. A runner with good speed at second can usually beat the shortstop to third, allowing the runner from first to move into scoring position at second base.

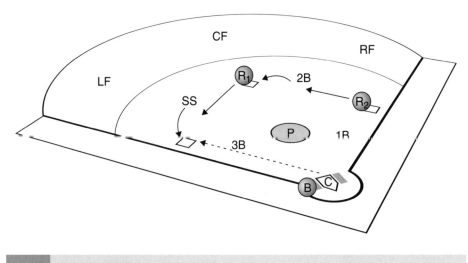

**11.1** Double steal.

# Hitting Bunts

Another way to get runners into scoring position is to use a sacrifice bunt. If the runner on first isn't fast enough to steal second, a relatively safe way to move her over is to bunt. How often a team bunts with a runner on first depends on several things: how good a bunter the batter is; how likely it is the runner will be safe if the bunt is successful; what the defense is expecting; how well the defense would be able to throw out the runner at second; and how the game is going. If the game appears to be a close pitchers' duel, moving the runner into scoring position is a wise decision.

A drag bunt is an important offensive weapon for hitters who have good running speed and can get on base. If the first and third basemen are playing back, even with two outs, and the batter is able to get the drag bunt down, then often this simple play to get on base is the best move.

A less common bunt is the squeeze play (figure 11.2). A team that has a quick runner on third and a good bunter at the plate can surprise the defense with a squeeze bunt, in which the hitter lays down the bunt as the runner tries to steal home. The runner on third must get a good jump off third, and the batter must not show his intention to bunt too early. Typically a squeeze bunt is used when it appears that one run may be the difference in the game, especially in the late innings.

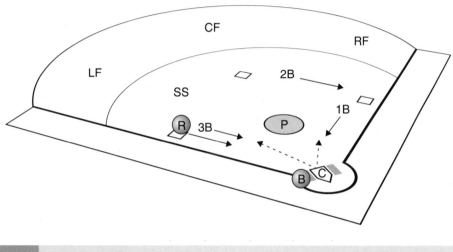

**11.2**    **Squeeze play.**

# Hitting Sacrifice Flys

With fewer than two outs, a runner has the option of tagging up on a fly ball and attempting to advance to the next base. In certain situations, tagging up makes the most sense. Rarely should a runner at first base tag up, unless she is extremely quick, the ball is hit deep into the outfield, and it is especially important to move into scoring position. A runner on second should tag up on any deep fly ball to right field or the right–centerfield gap. Even if the ball isn't caught, the runner should be able to score easily.

Scoring from third base on a fly ball is an easy way to get a run without a hit. The batter must realize her role with a runner on third—hit a ball hard somewhere into the outfield. The batter should look for a pitch that is a littler higher in the strike zone, but she also needs to be cautious and not get jammed on an inside pitch. When the ball is hit, the runner at third should immediately recognize that she needs to tag up. The runner must watch for the ball to be caught before running for home. Only the coach should decide the runner should not go home.

When the ball is hit into foul territory, a defensive player needs to make a diving catch, or a defensive player needs to make an over-the-shoulder catch, the runner should look to tag up. When an infielder makes an over-the-shoulder catch while running away from the infield, a quick runner often can tag and easily advance.

# Using Short-Game Opportunities

A left-handed slap hitter who comes to bat with runners on base can choose from a variety of strategies for getting on base and moving runners into scoring position. When there is a runner on first and a slap hitter at bat, the defense must decide who will cover second on a steal. If the shortstop covers second, the best option would be to use a hit and run, with the slap hitter placing the ball toward the shortstop (figure 11.3). As the runner steals second, the shortstop plays more up the middle to cover the base, allowing a ground ball in that direction to get through the infield. If the second baseman covers second on a steal, the slap hitter should bunt the ball toward first base since the pitcher will have to cover the bunt down the first base line (figure 11.4).

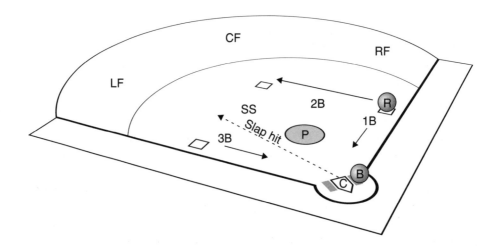

**11.3**   **Hit and run with slap hitter, runner on first.**

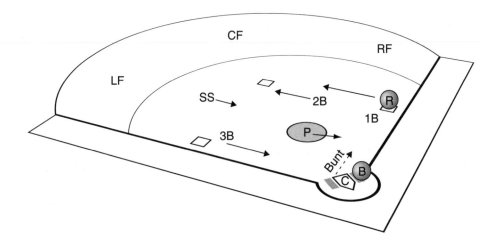

**11.4** **Bunt with slap hitter, runner on first.**

With a runner on second, the defense must cover third base on the steal. With a slap hitter at the plate, the third baseman will play closer to home, leaving the shortstop to cover third base on a steal. As the runner attempts to steal third, the slap hitter hits the ball toward the shortstop, who is out of position to cover third, and the runner can score easily on the base hit (figure 11.5).

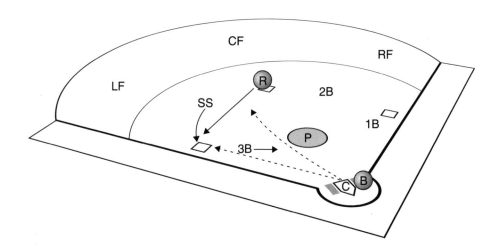

**11.5** **Ground ball to shortstop, runner on second.**

# Scouting the Opponent

Being able to recognize the abilities and strengths of your own team is the key to any offensive strategy. However, scouting a future opponent, either in another game or in a warm-up, allows the coach to create an even more thorough offensive game plan. It may be difficult for the coach to spend time away from preparing his team, but observing the defensive abilities of an opponent can play a major role in game situations. It may even determine which players will be in the lineup for a game.

One of the first areas of a defense to evaluate is the catcher. Because the catcher is involved in so many plays, she is a critical link to watch for greater offensive success. If she has a great throwing arm during the warm-up, you can bet it won't change during the game. Your coach may want to see how accurate she is by testing her early in a game, but if her throws looked accurate during the warm-up, she most likely will play the same way. In addition to arm strength and accuracy, how long it takes the catcher to get rid of a ball is an important factor. This can be timed using a stopwatch. Usually from the time she catches the ball until it reaches the target is a good standard. However, the release time can also be isolated, from the time she catches the ball until she releases it. If your team is good at baserunning, knowing these qualities can make or break your strategy.

When evaluating a catcher, your coach will also look at his footwork and quickness. Does he like to get down in the dirt and block the ball, or does he tend to put his mitt down and hope the ball goes in it? If a catcher tends to try to catch the ball when it is thrown into the dirt, you can often take extra bases because the ball will likely get away from him. Also, what kind of leader is he on the field? If he seems to be quiet and lets others tell him what to do, it is a sure sign that he is a weak link and can be taken advantage of.

Another important part of scouting an opponent is to observe the outfielders. If you or your coach notice an outfielder with a weak or inaccurate throwing arm, your team can plan on taking an extra base when balls are hit in her direction. Watch the outfielders' running speed, and note how comfortable they are catching balls while on the run or going back toward the fence. Many deep fly balls that should be caught end up as base hits because of poor outfield play.

Watch the first and third basemen for how quickly they move to get a ball and how soon they can make a throw. This can be a crucial factor in your bunt strategy. If either of these players, or even the pitcher, has difficulty fielding and throwing the ball on a bunt, then your coach will want to make that part of your game plan.

Some players look good in the warm-up because they possess good skills and athletic ability, but when the pressure is on during a game, they have a difficult time. Look for players that tend to get frustrated by a mistake because it will generally lead to more. A good offensive team is always looking to take advantage of a defensive weakness. Most players are good enough to make the play without pressure, but look for opportunities when a mental mistake is made. This is when most players relax for a second and lose focus.

Practicing offensive tactics and game situations can be difficult, depending on the number of players on the team. Gamelike situations in practice, using the players available, assess how strategies work and create a stressful environment that simulates a game. Most teams don't have enough players to hold full scrimmages, with nine players on two different teams and each position filled by someone who will play there in an actual game. Your coach needs to be creative and use specific drills to rehearse the strategy being developed.

## CENTER TOSS ON FIELD

Using a coach to toss balls to a hitter with a defensive team in the field can be the best simulation to a real game that you can hope for. By using the coach, the hitters have a better chance of being successful. If a pitcher is used, there will be a lot more hitters missing pitches and typically more balls thrown by the pitcher. To practice specific strategies, such as bunts or hit and runs, runners should be in the proper positions, but the defensive team should not know what is going to happen so it appears more gamelike. The coach tossing to the hitter can either make the drill more easy or difficult depending on the specific needs.

## TWO STRIKE AT-BAT

Once you get two strikes as a batter, it becomes increasingly difficult to get a hit. For one, it creates more stress, and two, the pitcher will typically not throw the ball down the middle of the plate. This is a good situation for you to practice before it happens in a game. It could be with live pitching, a coach throwing center toss, or even a machine simulating a pitch. Whichever drill is used, step into the batter's box as if you had two strikes. If you watch strike three or swing and miss, then your turn is over and someone else steps in. By increasing the urgency of hitting the ball, you tend to be a more aggressive hitter and learn which balls you can hit well and which ones you can't.

## MACHINE GAME

If you don't have a pitching machine, you can do this drill with live pitching or a coach throwing center toss as well. Each player receives a chart that lists a series of offensive actions you might perform in a game. This list usually includes a sacrifice bunt, squeeze bunt, hit and run, and so on. Use the chart to keep your score for the entire drill. If you perform the skill perfectly you get three points for that pitch. If you perform it partially you receive one point, and if you don't perform well at all, then you lose a point. Keep these charts over an extended period, and use them to compare your scores early in the season and then after practicing for a while.

# Defensive Tactics

**A**s with offensive players, defensive players can come in all shapes and sizes. Depending on skills, a player may have a number of defensive options on each play. By knowing your own strengths and weaknesses, you can help your team by optimally positioning yourself in the field to make the play, based on the batter and the game situation. For example, an outfielder who has great foot speed can play a more shallow position with a power hitter at bat than an outfielder who doesn't have very good speed. An outfielder who has good arm strength can play a little deeper with a runner on second because the outfielder will be able to throw the runner out if the runner tries to score on a base hit.

All defensive players must react to the ability of the hitter and the game situation. If you know the location and speed of the next pitch, you can anticipate where the batter is likely to hit the ball. You should also learn the tendencies of the hitter. Some hitters tend to pull the ball no matter where the pitch is thrown, and you can position yourself accordingly. Pay attention to other batters' swings during the pregame warm-up, in the on-deck circle, and at the plate. The information you gather from observing their tendencies will pay huge dividends during the game.

# Finding a Position

Finding the position that suits you best is an inexact science and can be a difficult process for any player. You may have one idea about where you should play, and your coach may have another. For example, you may think you are a shortstop, but the coach tells you to play centerfield. Remember that coaches look at the team differently than players do. Each team has different needs to fill depending on the other players on the team. The best approach is to trust the coach, but ask why she thinks this position is best for you and the team. If you want to play another position, express those feelings; find out what you can do to improve your skills and possibly play in your preferred position in the future.

Coaches look for certain skills and characteristics in players for particular positions. A team may not have the perfect player for a particular position, but the coach will evaluate the players who are available and find the best fit.

Most coaches prefer outfielders who are fast and can cover a lot of ground to run down fly balls and cut off base hits in the gap. An outfielder also needs a strong throwing arm because he will need to make longer throws to the infield. A good outfielder also communicates well with the other outfielders and the infielders to prevent collisions on fly balls. Typically the centerfielder is in charge of the outfield and is the leader of the group. The centerfielder covers the most territory by running down balls in both right– and left–centerfield gaps (figure 12.1). Typically the right fielder needs to have the strongest throwing arm of the outfielders because she has a longer

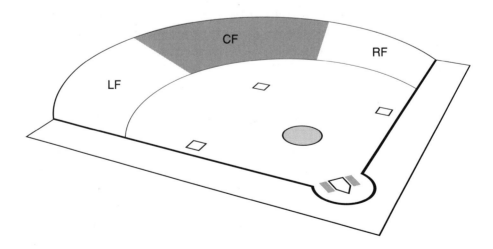

**12.1** **Areas of coverage for outfielders.**

throw to third base. A left fielder must have a quicker release on the throw and be sure-handed to prevent runners from scoring on base hits.

First basemen can be right or left handed, although left-handed first basemen have the advantage of more easily cutting off ground balls between themselves and the second baseman. The first baseman must have good hands to be able to scoop the ball out of the dirt. She must not be afraid to catch the ball while the runner is approaching first base. Although usually not as quick footed as most infielders, the first baseman must still be able to cover bunts. Usually the first baseman is the cutoff for home on hits into the outfield.

Second basemen are usually quick footed, but they do not require the strongest throwing arms since it is a shorter throw to first base. The second baseman must be able to cover first on a bunt and must not be afraid of making a tough play when the runner is approaching the base.

Usually the shortstop is the most consistent infielder and has the greatest range for fielding ground balls. He needs a strong throwing arm to make the longer throw to first base. Shortstops usually are also responsible for being cutoffs. A shortstop must be able to concentrate on catching the throw from the catcher during a steal attempt and making the tag on a runner sliding in hard.

For a third baseman, most coaches look for a quick-footed infielder who can handle most bunts. She also must be fearless; the ball can be hit at great speed toward third, and the third baseman stands much closer to home plate. Third base is often called the hot corner because of the difficult and hard-hit ground balls that come that way. The third baseman must have a quick release on the throw to first.

Probably the two most physically and mentally difficult positions on the field are pitcher and catcher. Both positions are involved in every play and require focus and concentration throughout the game. The pitcher and catcher require specific skills and physical abilities.

The catcher must be a tough-minded individual who enjoys being in charge. He is responsible for calling pitches, positioning fielders, calling out plays, and working with the pitcher. Most catchers have a strong throwing arm, although a catcher who can release the ball quickly can be just as effective as one who throws harder. A good catcher cannot be afraid of stopping pitches that bounce in the dirt or catching a throw as a runner slides into home plate. He must be willing to handle the physical punishment that comes from catching every pitch and taking the occasional foul tip off the face mask, elbow, or shoulder.

The pitcher is the most watched player on the field, so she must be able to handle pressure and perform well when the game is on the line. A pitcher must practice pitching skills year-round. A good pitcher does not let her skills diminish. The pitcher also must exude confidence, be a leader on the field, and communicate the proper play. She also fields bunts, backs up throws to bases, and makes the occasional throw to first base. Pitchers who can throw the ball with great velocity are usually quite tall and use their height to generate ball speed. Pitchers who rely on ball movement more than speed are usually much smaller. They keep hitters off balance by changing speeds and mixing up the location rather than throwing hard.

Table 12.1 summarizes the defensive positions on the field and the qualities players need to assume the various roles.

**Table 12.1**

## DEFENSIVE POSITIONS AND SKILLS

| Defensive position | Primary skill | Other skills |
| --- | --- | --- |
| Pitcher | Pitching | Fielding and throwing to bases |
| Catcher | Catching pitches; blocking and framing pitches | Throwing to bases and receiving throws from position players |
| First baseman | Catching the ball at first | Throwing to bases and fielding hit and bunted balls |
| Second baseman | Fielding hit balls | Throwing to and covering bases, especially first base on bunts |
| Shortstop | Fielding hit balls | Throwing to bases and taking charge of the infield |
| Third baseman | Handling bunts | Throwing to bases |
| Left fielder | Catching fly balls | Handling all types of ground balls and throwing to bases |
| Centerfielder | Running down fly balls in the gaps | Leading the outfield, fielding all types of ground balls, and throwing to bases |
| Right fielder | Catching fly balls | Throwing out runners who are trying to go from first to third on a base hit; fielding ground balls |

One of the most exciting aspects of fastpitch softball is the variety of defensive strategies and options available. Defensive alignment changes constantly during a game, depending on the location of base runners, the tendencies of the hitter, or the game situation. Good defensive positioning gives even a weak defensive player the chance to make the play.

# Defending Bunts

Typically the third and first basemen (the corners) cover the infield for most bunts. When a sacrifice bunt situation exists, the corners move closer to the batter to decrease their distance to the potential bunt (figure 12.2). The pitcher is usually involved in bunt coverage as well, but primarily the pitcher stays back to handle any push bunt attempt that gets past the first or third baseman. Whenever possible, the third baseman should field the bunt because he has a better angle of approach to the ball, giving the third baseman a better chance to field the bunt and complete the throw to first base.

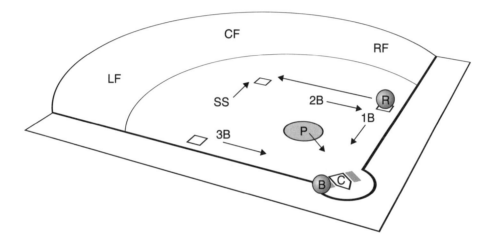

**12.2** Corners move in close in anticipation of a sacrifice bunt.

The second baseman generally covers first base on a bunt attempt. The second baseman should take a direct angle to first base and get there quickly. The second baseman's left foot hits the inside portion of first base, and she sets in good athletic position, ready to catch the throw. If a poor throw pulls the second baseman off the bag into the runner's path, the second baseman should move across the base to receive the throw and avoid the oncoming runner.

In a sacrifice bunt situation with a runner on first, whichever corner doesn't get the ball should head to third base to prevent the runner from advancing further. Outfielders are also involved in the play; they back up the throw to first base and the potential throw to third or second.

Whenever possible, on a sacrifice bunt it is best to get the out at second base to keep the runner out of scoring position (figure 12.3).

The shortstop should recognize the bunt and set up facing home plate as if playing first base, with the right foot on second base. The short-stop stretches toward the throw and quickly gets out of the runner's way. It is a gamble to try to get the runner out at second since the runner will have a head start. Making the play depends on many factors including the runner's speed and the force of the bunt.

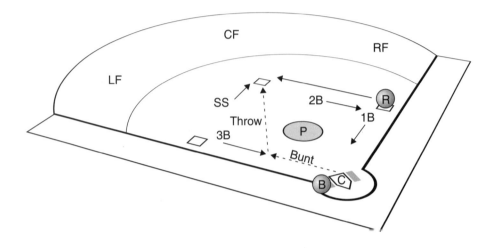

**12.3**   Getting the runner out at second on a sacrifice bunt.

# Defending First-and-Third Situations

With runners on first and third base, the defense has several options to prevent the runner on third from scoring on a steal by the runner at first. If your team is ahead by several runs, getting the runner out at second should be your primary focus. However if the game is close or it is late in the game, you must get an out or keep the runners from advancing.

The most popular play for this situation is to have the second baseman move between the pitcher and second base after the pitch is thrown. As the catcher makes the throw, the second baseman watches the runner at third to see if she is going to try to steal home. If the runner at third doesn't move, the second baseman lets the ball go through to the shortstop, who is covering second base, and the shortstop tags the runner at second (figure 12.4a). If the runner at third heads home on the throw, the second baseman cuts off the throw from the catcher and throws the ball home (figure 12.4b).

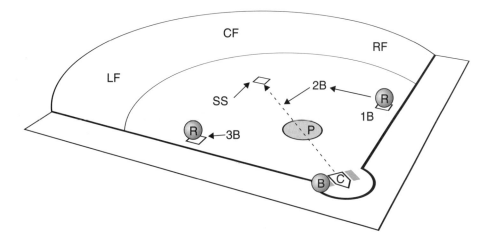

**12.4a**   **Runner at third stays at third and out is made at second.**

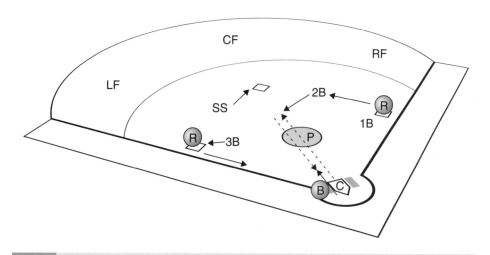

**12.4b**   **Runner at third runs toward home on the throw.**

Another popular play for defending a first-and-third situation is for the catcher to fake a throw to second and instead throw to third. Or the catcher could throw the ball to the shortstop, who then makes a play on the runner at third. Another option is for the catcher to throw the ball hard toward second base, but the pitcher intercepts the ball and makes a play on the runner at third. Whichever strategy is preferred, it is important to practice these plays many times before using them in a game.

# Defending Slap Hits

Defending the short game begins with proper positioning. If the batter is strictly a left-handed slap hitter, the outfielders can come in to within 20 feet (6.1 meters) of the infield grass (figure 12.5). However, understand that if the slap hitter chooses to hit away or slaps a ball in the gap, he may quickly circle the bases for a home run. The third and first basemen play up in bunt coverage position. Typically the second baseman comes up into the baseline, but some teams move the second baseman all the way up near the pitcher to field potential bunts.

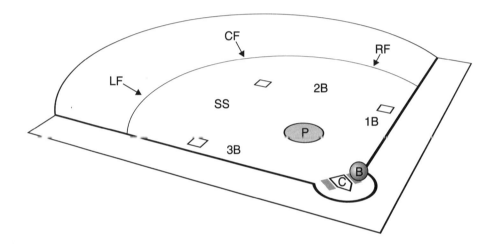

**12.5**    **Proper positioning for defending a slap hitter.**

The shortstop is the key player in defending a slap hitter. The shortstop moves up into the baseline between second and third. By moving up, she reduces the target area for the slap hitter. However since the shortstop is so close to the batter, she is vulnerable to a hard-hit ball. If the shortstop can't react to a sharply hit ball, she may need to stay back a little, but she still should slide slightly over toward the third base side.

Once positioned correctly, each defensive player must understand that charging the ball and making a quick throw are crucial for getting a slap hitter out. Most slap hitters reach first base in less than three seconds from the time they make contact with the ball. At practice, infielders should field and throw the ball to first in less than three seconds to prepare for defending a slap hitter in a game.

# Using Intentional Walks

At certain moments in a game, intentionally walking a batter is the smart thing to do. With one or two outs, runners on third and second, walking the batter creates a force situation at any base. An intentional walk also may lead to a double play from home to first if the batter being intentionally walked is a relatively slow runner. Your coach should scout the team you are playing to determine which players would be good candidates to walk. Usually the opponent's best hitter is walked, and a hitter that is easier to get out is pitched to.

The catcher signals the pitcher for an intentional walk, usually by standing up and holding an arm out away from the batter (see chapter 5, page 48). The pitcher aims for a spot in the empty batter's box, high enough for the catcher to handle the ball easily. As the ball is pitched, the catcher moves into position so he can easily catch the ball.

# Using Pitchouts and Pickoffs

Call a pitchout if it looks as if a runner is going to try to steal or if you want to run a pickoff play. The catcher signals for a pitchout while squatting in a regular stance. The pitcher aims for a spot in the empty batter's box, hopefully about shoulder height so the catcher can handle it easily. The pitcher should throw the ball with a lot of velocity to give the catcher more time to make the throw to get the stealing runner.

For a pickoff play during a steal, the catcher calls for the pitchout. If the runner is attempting to steal the base, the catcher should be in good position to make a throw to get the out.

If the catcher thinks a runner on first is taking too aggressive a lead, the catcher can call the pickoff play to try to throw out the runner at first. Either the first or second baseman can be asked to get back to first base before the runner gets there. Because the first baseman is in front of the runner in plain view, it is usually more successful to run a pickoff play with the second baseman covering the base (figure 12.6). This uses the element of surprise. As the pitcher releases the ball, the chosen player should break for first base and be ready to receive a quick throw from the catcher. Leave as little room as possible for the runner returning to the base.

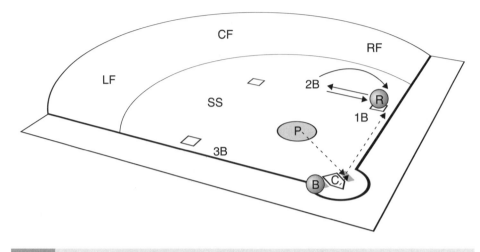

For a pickoff to second base, either the shortstop or second baseman can cover second. The pickoff to second base can be a risky play because of the long throw to second from home. Often a good base runner will try to get the defense to throw to second so the base runner can head for third. A better play than the pickoff may be to fake a throw to second to see if the runner really is trying to steal third.

With a runner at third base, either the shortstop can sneak in behind the runner or the third baseman can cover the base. Usually it is more successful to bring the shortstop over because the runner can see the third baseman. The runner may not realize that the shortstop has headed over to third.

# Backing Up Plays

One of the most important roles outfielders and pitchers fulfill is backing up throws to bases. Although this skill is not always noticed, it can save a run or even a game if a player backing up a play is in position to stop a poor throw.

The right fielder usually backs up throws to first base, the centerfielder backs up throws to second, and the left fielder backs up throws to third. In some circumstances, outfielders may need to cover other bases, so it is important for outfielders to keep moving and get in position to help whenever possible. The pitcher is responsible for backing up throws from the outfield to both third base and home.

When backing up a base, give yourself enough room to react to the ball if it bounces off a player's glove or the runner. Usually you should stay about 20 feet (6.1 meters) away from the base to be able to react properly.

# Executing Rundowns

A runner who strays a little too far from the base may get caught in a rundown. During a rundown, the base runner is stranded between two bases while the defense tries to tag her out. When a runner is trapped between bases, defensive players must remember that the runner is the one in trouble. Often defensive players begin to panic during rundowns; it is important to stay calm and keep the play simple. The goal of a rundown is to get an out, but if the runner ends up back at the original base, no harm was done.

The first point in a rundown is to note the starting point of the runner. You want to keep the runner from advancing to the next base. The player covering the next base should get the ball as soon as possible and sprint toward the runner, driving the runner back toward the original base. Once the runner turns back or gets close to the original base, the player covering the original base calls for the ball by yelling and raising his arms. Eventually the defensive player with the ball tags out the runner. It may take several throws before the defensive player with the ball is close enough to the runner to make the tag. If the defense allows the base runner to return to the original base, the defensive team is no worse off. The worse thing the defensive team can do during a rundown is let the runner advance a base.

# Executing Cutoffs and Relay Throws

When a ball is thrown from the outfield to the infield, a cutoff player should be in position to intercept the throw if the runner isn't trying to advance. The cutoff player is also responsible for keeping a poorly thrown ball from getting away. She should be in a direct line with the incoming throw. Usually the player covering the base will line up the cutoff player.

The shortstop is the cutoff for balls hit to left or centerfield if the throw comes to second base. The second baseman is the cutoff for balls hit to right field. Either cutoff should get in position slightly less than halfway between the outfielder and the base. For throws to third base, the shortstop is always the cutoff and should get in position accordingly. The first baseman is the cutoff for nearly every throw to home plate, both base hits and fly balls. The first baseman should be in position near the baseline, ready to catch the ball at the catcher's direction. If the catcher feels there won't be a play at home but there will be a play at another base, the first baseman must be ready to quickly change direction and throw to that base.

On a ground ball base hit to left field, the third baseman can turn and quickly get in position to handle the cutoff. Some teams use the first baseman, but it is extremely difficult for the first baseman to recognize the base hit and then get all the way across the field into position to make the play.

# Communicating on the Field

Communication is a crucial part of fastpitch softball. Good communication can prevent injuries as well as win ball games. Because the field is such a large space, both verbal and nonverbal communication is important.

Although you need to be loud enough for everyone to hear you, it is important that other players understand what you are saying as well. Keep the words short, and repeat them several times when calling across the field to another player. An outfielder calling for a fly ball can holler, "Mine, mine, mine!" to let everyone know she is catching the ball. By making calls loud and audible, players can avoid colliding with each other. If two players are calling for the ball, repeating the call several times alerts both players that someone is nearby. Based on preestablished rules, one player should back off.

A lot of communication happens before the play. The catcher may point to the shortstop to cover second base on a steal or move an outfielder slightly. As you play with the same group of people, you will develop more nonverbal communication. Everyone will be able to anticipate and understand what the others are thinking.

Communication on the field also allows players to concentrate on the upcoming play rather than the play that just happened or an at-bat from a previous inning. When a mistake is made, players tend to keep replaying it in their minds, distracting them from the current action on the field. Continually talking with teammates during the action makes it easier for everyone to forget the past mistakes and concentrate on the next play.

Another important area of communication is between the pitcher and catcher. The pitcher and catcher interact a lot, working together every play and agreeing on which pitch to throw. When things are going well on the field, the communication between pitcher and catcher is usually free and easy. The problems begin when something doesn't go well and tension is high. The catcher can be a calming influence on the pitcher. Depending on the personality of the pitcher and the game situation, a catcher may need to use different techniques with the pitcher. Usually the catcher is encouraging and reminds the pitcher of past successes, urging her to relax and let the team play behind her. The interaction between these two players is one of the most important relationships on the field.

Your coach must communicate with the team before, during, and after the game. Before the game, the coach sets the tone of the game. He must recognize the team's preparedness. Once the game begins, the coach needs to pass along signals and strategies to the players and make positional changes depending on the game situation. Because the coach cannot go onto the field all the time, the team must practice understanding his hand signals. After the game, the coach should review both the positive and negative aspects of play and get the team ready for the next game.

*Give it a go*

Practicing defensive situations is an important part of any team's preparation before a game. Although you can never quite re-create a game situation in practice, the closer you come the better a team will be prepared.

## BASE RUNNER DRILL

Set up a game situation with runners on base and a runner near home to simulate a batter. It is often more effective if a coach hits the ball from home plate to control the location and speed of the hit more easily. Try to find weaknesses in the defense that opponents may try to exploit. The coach should hit balls to various parts of the field using different combinations of runners and outs.

## CENTER TOSS WITH DEFENSE

Set up a regular defense with a coach throwing to batters instead of a pitcher. By having the coach toss to batters, more action is created and the defense can see the ball come off the bat, just as in a real game. Move runners into different positions and change the outs to simulate areas the team needs to pay special attention to.

## STOPWATCH INFIELD

Use a stopwatch to time how long it takes infielders to field and throw the ball to the appropriate base. Call out times to turn this into a competitive drill. This is a good way to see how quickly a team can turn double plays.

## SCRIMMAGE DRILL

Divide the group into two equal teams with a coach acting as the pitcher. Depending on the number of players, the teams may or may not have enough people to fill all positions. Simulate gamelike conditions and create a competitive environment, with the winning team being rewarded in some way. Play a game with standard rules, or switch things up to move it along by starting each inning with two outs or having two strikes on each batter. You can also start each inning with a runner on second base. If the defensive team stops the runner from scoring, the players receive a special award.

# About the Writer

**Rick Noren** has compiled an outstanding 320-79 (.802) record in his 10 seasons as the Pacific Lutheran University fastpitch head coach. The Lutes have won eight conference titles, finished in the top five in the country three times, and led the nation in winning percentage twice during Noren's tenure.

Additionally, Noren teaches several activity classes at PLU as well as a softball and baseball theory class for coaching students. Every year he conducts clinics for softball coaches and players throughout the Pacific Northwest.

Noren earned his bachelor's degree in exercise science from Western Washington University and his master's degree in athletic administration from Pacific Lutheran University. Rick's wife, Leanne, is the PLU pitching coach. The Norens and their children, Kyle, Joel, and Leah, live in Tacoma, Washington.

# Master softball's essentials with *Softball Skills & Drills!*

**Softball Skills & Drills**
Series DVD
Approx. 120-minute DVD
ISBN 0-7360-6025-1

*Softball Skills & Drills* book/video package
224 pages/approx. 40-minute videos
ISBN 0-7360-4029-3
ISBN PAL 0-7360-4030-7

Learn how to perform and improve your hitting, bunting, slap hitting, baserunning, fielding, throwing, pitching, and catching skills from Judi Garman, one of the top coaches in NCAA history. Packed with 170 drills and over 190 photos and illustrations, *Softball Skills & Drills* covers more than the Xs and Os. This practical handbook is loaded with tips that will speed your skill development.

See the techniques and drills in action with the companion video series or DVD:

- *Hitting and Baserunning* covers everything from correctly gripping the bat to building a powerful swing
- *Fielding* covers everything from proper throwing technique to fielding a backhand or fly ball
- *Pitching and Catching* presents a variety of drills to improve technique

Each skill is carefully explained and properly demonstrated, often shown repeatedly in slow motion and at different angles for maximum effect.

Whether you are a beginning softball player or the coach of an all-star team, the *Softball Skills & Drills* book/video package or book and DVD is sure to take you to the championship level!

To place your order,
U.S. customers call TOLL FREE

# 1-800-747-4457

In Canada call 1-800-465-7301
In Australia call 08 8277 1555
In New Zealand call (09) 448 1207
In Europe call +44 (0) 113 255 5665

or visit **www.HumanKinetics.com**

**HUMAN KINETICS**
*The Premier Publisher for Sports & Fitness*
P.O. Box 5076, Champaign, IL 61825-5076
www.HumanKinetics.com